THE BIBLE AND THE CHURCH
An Approach to Scripture

WESTMINSTER GUIDES TO THE BIBLE
Edwin M. Good, General Editor

THE BIBLE
AND
THE CHURCH

An Approach to Scripture

by
SAMUEL TERRIEN

Philadelphia
THE WESTMINSTER PRESS

Contents

Preface

WHAT is the Bible? How is it properly used? What is it all about? Questions like these are by no means easily answered, nor are all the answers given to them by former generations entirely acceptable today. In every generation, the Bible must undergo the scrutiny of that generation's questions. In every generation, the Bible becomes the word of God in relation to that generation's problems.

But each generation must grapple with the *Bible,* not merely with its own ideas about the Bible. To understand this book in our own day must involve understanding the book on its own terms as well as understanding the most profound movements of the modern mind. There is, then, a kind of double process of comprehending the Bible. On the one hand is the book itself, sitting " out there," which we must study as a book coming from a particular culture in a particular time. On the other hand is the church — ourselves — " right here," listening to the ancient word in a world of which the ancient writers could not have dreamed. How is the gap between these two to be bridged?

Professor Terrien applies his mind to this question. Setting out, on the one hand, the facts that the thoughtful reader of the Bible must know about it, he illuminates it in its own terms. Setting out, on the other hand, the ways in which our

7

minds function, he suggests what we are and what we are concerned with. But central to his concern is the crossing of the gap between us and the Bible, the faith that leaps across and hears God — astonishingly! — speaking there, the worship that springs from and carries us to the Word of God.

The Westminster Guides to the Bible grew in the first instance out of the stimulus of the Layman's Theological Library. If, we thought, laymen in the church could be so eloquently encouraged to be theologians, why could they not be encouraged to be Bible scholars as well? In the modern resurgence of serious thinking about the Christian faith, the study of the Bible has played a major role. But the methods and results of this recent study have not been made available to laymen.

The Westminster Guides to the Bible seek to fill this gap. In nine brief volumes, we introduce the riches of the major portions of the Bible and of the period " between the Testaments." The writers share the conviction that the Bible lies at the heart of Christianity, and that it is imperative that laymen be aided to take a firm grip on Biblical faith. We are certain that this means no denial of the mind. On the contrary, the Bible demands the utmost our minds can give it, and searching study repays our efforts with new insight.

Of course, we are primarily concerned with the Bible, not with our books about it. We hope that the reader will have his Bible in hand as he reads these books, and that he will turn to it again with greater anticipation when he has finished.

And it is with laymen, who are the backbone of the church, that we are concerned. We have written, not for scholars already learned, but for those who seek to learn. We are certain that no wishy-washy faith, no cheap " religiousness," is wanted. In the vigor of Biblical faith we trust that the reader will find invigoration. If so, the church of Christ will be served.

EDWIN M. GOOD

Introduction

THE Bible is not a book but a library (in Greek, *ta biblia,* "the books"). Thirty-nine of them, written in Hebrew and a bit of Aramaic between 1000 and 150 B.C., form the "Books of the Old Covenant" (or "Old Testament"). Twenty-seven others, composed in Greek between A.D. 50 and 150, constitute the "Books of the New Covenant" (or "New Testament"). Why should such a motley of ancient and foreign documents concern modern man?

The answers are many, but one stands out. The church finds in the Bible not only the history of her origins but also the controlling factor of her faith. Hence the title of this volume: THE BIBLE AND THE CHURCH.

In the stories of the Old and New Testaments, and supremely in the picture of God that dominates the entire Bible, Christians discover themselves alive and wanted. They learn that the universe is a *cosmos,* that is to say, a monument of harmony and beauty. They find out that mankind has a history, that is to say, an organic unity that moves toward a goal.

To be sure, Christians do not ignore the other foundations of culture — literature and philosophy, science and the arts — but they ascribe to the Bible a unique place because it nurtures in them a reality which they are not ashamed to call "the living Christ." Luther's picturesque statement was: "The Bible is the cradle of Christ." Some such affirmation must be made if one attempts to seek the secret of the vitality that the Bible has enjoyed for nearly two millennia. At the same time, such an affirmation can be made only by those who enter the strange world of the Bible and read there no longer an ancient tale but their own story. At that moment, Homer and Shakespeare may continue to thrill them, Rembrandt and Bach to delight and inspire them, Darwin and Freud to enlighten them, but the Bible does for them all this and more. It undermines selfishness and grants selfhood, thereby transforming existence into life.

Together with the Lord's Supper, from which it cannot be divorced, the Bible is the locus where the reality of a Presence binds them together into a community that defies time and mortality. The Bible is the true locale of the church, an explosive society that violates the laws of sociology and nature. Thus, the Bible has a disruptive side, which threatens the security of individuals and nations — and churches! For this reason, many readers of the Bible soon become ill at ease, and they throw the book away or place it piously on some holy shelf, the better to forget its menace.

One favorite way to ignore the Bible is to say that it is old. Emily Dickinson conveyed the attitude of many when she wrote:

> "The Bible is an antique volume
> Written by faded men
> At the suggestion of Holy Spectres."

We shall recognize that many barriers separate us from the "antique volume," and we shall not minimize the intellectual difficulties we confront when we attempt to read it.

In the *first* place, the sixty-six books of the Bible were written in the course of thirty generations. We should not expect to find in these books a unified view of man, of life, or of God. Indeed, we should be surprised if we did not discover in their pages a host of repetitions and contradictions. The amazing fact that emerges from the study of the Bible is its unity in depth, under the surface of its diversity.

In the *second* place, the sixty-six books have not been preserved in the order of their publication. For example, Genesis (fifth century B.C.) appeared after Amos (who lived in the eighth century B.C.). The letters of Paul already circulated among the Christian communities of the Roman Empire before any of the four Gospels was written.

In the *third* place, many of the sixty-six books were not written down on parchment until long after they had already " existed " in an oral form. Men gathered around the campfires of the desert or at the shrines of Canaan, and they chanted the stories of the exodus and sang the saga of the patriarchs. Yet, the book of Genesis did not receive its final form until centuries of singing had passed. Likewise, the " good news " of the life and death of Jesus was told with liturgical solemnity and in a fixed oral form before the letters of Paul were penned, and it continued to be proclaimed orally for years afterward. Obviously, a knowledge of history is indispensable to the understanding of these documents.

In the *fourth* place, the Biblical books include a considerable variety of literary styles, not only from book to book, but also within almost every writing of the Old Testament and many writings of the New Testament. Legends and myths are placed, without transition or warning, side by side with poems, family genealogies, royal archives, and eyewitness accounts of historical events. Administrative rules, criminal and civil codes, religious prescriptions and moral commands, are mixed with folk ballads and visions of the end of history. Such chaotic disarray, of course, baffles the modern reader, but a study of the growth of the Biblical books may place them in clear perspective.

In the *fifth* place, traditions preserved in many of these books arose in concrete situations of history. For example, the story of creation in Gen., ch. 2, is far older than that in Gen., ch. 1. The older account was told in a time of national prosperity (tenth century B.C.), when David had defeated all his enemies. Thus the growing nationalism of Israel had to be sobered by the reminder that God alone is strong and that man is dust. The later story, in Gen., ch. 1, was told during the Babylonian exile (sixth century B.C.), when the nation had come to complete humiliation and political extinction. Thus the despair of the Jews had to be comforted by the faith that man was created in the image of God to be the vice-regent of the earth. Again, The Gospel According to Matthew was written chiefly for Christians of Jewish origin, probably in Antioch or in Asia Minor, whereas The Gospel According to Luke was composed for Christians of Greek extraction. The cultural differences between these two groups explain many features of the respective Gospels.

In the *sixth* place, the Bible comes from a distant age. Moses and the prophets, Jesus and the apostles, Paul and those to whom he wrote, knew nothing of the science of Newton or Einstein, even less of such modern sciences as psychology, biochemistry, or astrophysics. Should we not be prepared to find in the Bible a prescientific view of nature and of man? Should we be astonished to read that the universe was created in six days a few thousand years ago, that serpents eat dust, or that illness is wrought by seven or even a hundred demons in a single individual?

In the *seventh* place, these writings come not only from a distant age but also from the ancient Near East. They do not reflect the Greek spirit from which Western civilization largely emerged, but rather a Semitic, and more especially a Hebraic, way of thinking and speaking. Jesus was born a Jew, and he spoke Aramaic, a language closely akin to Hebrew. Intellectually he is much more closely related to Jeremiah than to Socrates. And while the writings of the New Testament were composed in Greek, most of their authors thought in the molds of the Hebrew and Aramaic languages. Such words as " fear," " love," or " justice " did not convey to them what they commonly connote to us. Again, the Biblical writers held to the notion of a collective personality in time as well as in space, which permitted them to hold to a strong sense of individuality without losing sight of social responsibility. They alone in the ancient world had a sense of history. They were aware of the " ongoingness " of the true Israel through the ages. They belonged to a society that transcended generations, in which the fathers long dead and — more extraordinary still — the sons yet unborn were concretely and realistically present. We have to adapt ourselves to such a mentality in order to grasp the meaning of the world " church " and of the sacrament of the Lord's Supper.

Finally, almost half of the Old Testament and many parts of the New are couched in a poetic style. Emotion infuses the phrases under the stylized forms. A sense of passionate urgency animates the speakers, whether Moses, the prophets, Jesus, or Paul. Their words are not mere vehicles of information; they are sensuous instruments of music that " contract the immensities " and capture the hearers. They penetrate to the will as well as to the mind. The prophets and the apostles were poets in the full sense of the word, for they did not play with words: they received them. The traditional language of the church attempted to express this when it said that they were " the inspired bearers of the Word." Now, poetry is not

readily accessible to casual acquaintance. Even less so is poetry
that must be read in translation. Here is perhaps the highest
hurdle for the reader of the Bible to leap. But he who will
open up all his faculties afresh may glance there, even if only
in a mirror, at

> " those gigantic shadows
> Which futurity casts upon the present."

Some of the difficulties we have just reviewed may be re-
moved by a study of the historical circumstances in which the
Bible was written and has come down to us through the centuries. But no book on the Bible can take the place of the
Book itself. And the Book itself is only a means for that mysterious season when any man or woman, aware of ephemeral-
ity, is met by his Maker and ushered into a company where
existence receives a quality of eternity.

The nuclear age will be called " post-Christian " unless the
church receives a new vitality. " We are still waiting, and I am
waiting," wrote Albert Camus, an existential atheist, " for a
rally of all those who refuse to be dogs, and are resolved to
pay the price."

CHAPTER 1 | *The People, the Presence,
and the Word*

THE Bible is a dead book unless it is read by a living church. Likewise, the church is a dead institution unless it is corrected and reformed in every age by a living Bible. The interaction that holds the Bible and the church in vital relationship can be seen from the history of their common origin.

I

The church emerged upon the historical scene at Jerusalem in A.D. 30, and it soon spread to all the provinces of the Roman Empire. One could say that, in some respects, the church was at first a Jewish sect, but such a statement would oversimplify the complexity of the situation. Christianity was born when Jesus and his disciples restated, against the official Judaism of their times, the dynamic vitality of ancient Hebraic faith.

Although Judaism is the offspring of Hebraism, one should make a clear distinction between the two of them. The religion of the Jews at the dawn of Christianity was by and large quite different from the faith of their ancestors, the ancient Hebrews.

The " Jews " did not appear before the year 587 B.C., when the " Judeans," or " Judahites," who had survived the destruction of the kingdom of " Judah " were deported to Babylon. The first " Jews " were the " Judeans " who refused to die as a

tightly knit society, although they had lost the usual supports
of national distinctiveness, such as territory, religious shrines,
and political government. The survival of the Judeans as Jews
constitutes one of the most extraordinary events of history.

If we inquire into the causes of this event, we discover a
number of reasons, the most important of which appears to be
a specifically religious one: the influence of the great prophets,
especially Jeremiah (626–580 B.C.) and Ezekiel (592–570 B.C.).
While these two men had a great deal in common, it is possible to state that Jeremiah led almost directly to Christianity,
and that Ezekiel was the father of Palestinian Judaism. Back
of them, however, stood the long inheritance of Moses and the
ancient Hebrews, in the second millennium B.C. Our inquiry
takes us, therefore, farther and farther into the distant past.

The ancient Hebrews did not form a nation in the usual
sense. They traced their origins to one man, Abraham, through
whom " all the families of the earth would be blessed and bless
each other " (Gen. 12:3). Alone in the ancient world, including the later Greeks and Romans, the Hebrews were conscious of a united mankind.

During the thirteenth century B.C., probably around 1275, a
group of Abraham's descendants, enslaved by Egypt in the
delta of the Nile, escaped oppression under the leadership of
Moses and formed in the desert of Sinai a religious federa-
tion. Bound to Yahweh by a " covenant," they became aware of
forming " a royal priesthood and a holy nation " (Ex. 19:6).

It was this awareness which the early Christians inherited,
so that The First Letter of Peter, at the end of the first century
A.D., describing the mission of the church to the world, could
do no better than to quote the covenant formula of the ancient Hebrews: " You are a chosen race, a royal priesthood,
a holy nation, God's own people " (I Peter 2:9).

A royal priesthood: this expression describes the specific

character of Hebraism and of the church, as well as their function in history. It presupposes three elements: a People, a Presence, and a Word. The people existed only on account of the presence of God in their midst, but this presence was inseparable from the proclamation and the fulfillment of his word.

II

In the ancient Near East, priests claimed to administer " the sacred " at the shrines of the gods. They formed a hierarchy apart from the common man. They offered sacrifices, performed rituals, pronounced prayers, dispensed oracles, and generally interpreted the " divine " will for the masses.

Kings usually enjoyed priestly status and fulfilled priestly functions, or else they governed with the support of the priests. Thus kingship and priesthood represented the two pillars of order in the early societies of history. Unfortunately, such an order was often imposed by fear and brute force. Gods were concerned with the welfare of kings and their dynasties, not with the populace. There was no concept of " peoplehood."

For the ancient Hebrews, on the contrary, religion was the responsibility of the entire nation, for Yahweh was the God, not of a monarch or a hierarchy, but of a *people*. The Hebrew slaves who had made bricks in Egypt for the Pharaoh, a " divine king," suddenly became the " slaves " of the Lord of heaven and earth. Their " service " to him was the sign of their freedom in history. They were free men because they belonged to him. " They are my slaves." (Lev. 25:42.) Those who had been a " no-people " became now, by covenant, " a royal priesthood, a holy nation."

While Egyptian and Mesopotamian kingdoms were constituted around monarchs or dynasties, with the apparatus of priests at the top of the social structure, the Hebrews formed a corporate solidarity of service. In its original sense, the expression *priesthood of all believers* meant the commitment of every member of the holy community. With the ancient Hebrews, the concept of priesthood received an altogether new and revolutionary meaning. The entire people, extending from generation to generation until the end of history, served the Master of that history. They did not serve a national deity, the "spirit" of some mountaintop, or any natural force like the sun or rain. They were not subjected to any king or potentate. They were the subjects of the King of all kings and potentates: "I have broken the bands of your yoke, and made you walk upright! " (Lev. 26:13.)

As the sons of the Hebrews conquered the Land of Canaan, however, they compromised with the cultures of the ancient Near East. The monarchy under David and Solomon corrupted the ideal of a holy people. Economic and political oppression split the nation into the Northern Kingdom of Israel and the Southern Kingdom of Judah (922 B.C.). Bitter hatred and social instability marked the life of the two states; the Northern Kingdom ended under the onslaught of the Assyrians (722 B.C.), while the Southern Kingdom was crushed in its turn by the Babylonians (587 B.C.). Yet, a handful of Judeans, exiled in Babylon, preserved against all odds their religious and national identity. They became the Jews. Once again, the question must be asked: What is the reason for this unique power of survival?

III

In order to grasp in their depth the historical forces that transformed *Hebraism* into *Judaism,* we must look at the second element implied in the notion of "royal priesthood," namely, the *presence* of God in the midst of his people.

All the ancient cults affirmed the presence of some deity in their shrines. For the Hebrews, however, Yahweh had placed the sun in the skies and made the dry land a theater fit for the inhabitation of man. He transcended all national interest and geographical limits. At the same time, he manifested his presence to Moses and to the people in a concrete manner. Memories of these manifestations told of signs in nature: a flame within a bush (Ex. 3:2), a cloud and a "thick darkness" on a mountaintop (Ex. 19:9, 16). Behind these signs, however, the proximity of the holy God was the genuine experience that gave the Hebrews their knowledge of themselves as a holy people: "I brought you unto myself!" (Ex. 19:4).

Unto myself! This is the cardinal reality that infused an amorphous amalgamation of slaves with an organic sense of purpose in history. Their exodus became a procession toward their God. The Passover celebrated far less their liberation than their ushering in to the Presence. Communion with Yahweh was the principle of "peoplehood." The Presence created the People.

Moreover, Yahweh was not conceived as a deity who sits in a temple. His worship was imageless. Such a thing was unique in antiquity. For Yahweh did not "sit" in a shrine, like the images of gold or marble that symbolized a static society with an arrested structure, a frozen hierarchy, or an immutable dynasty. He "walked with his people." Divine Presence was endowed with a dynamic quality without parallel in the ancient religions. It bore within itself the seed of historical growth.

Nevertheless, with the conquest of the Land of Canaan, and especially the corruption of the monarchy, the notion of Presence, like that of People, became radically transformed. Solomon built in Jerusalem a temple of cedar that looked like a Phoenician shrine for the worship of the sun. To be sure, he tried to prevent misunderstanding, for he said: "The sun!

Yahweh hath set in the heavens, and he hath promised to sojourn in thick darkness " (I Kings 8:12).

By preserving the nomadic idea of " sojourn " and recalling the "thick darkness" of nomadic days, Solomon attempted to avoid a confusion between a Presence that offers itself to man but remains free and a presence that man claims to enclose in a manufactured container for his eventual use and manipulation. But the second sentence had a disturbing sound: " I have built for thee a lofty mansion, a place for thee to sit in for ever " (I Kings 8:13).

This represented a direct violation of the old ways of Hebraism, which the prophet Nathan had recalled to David a few years earlier: "Thus says Yahweh, . . . 'I do not sit, . . . I walk!'" (II Sam. 7:5-6). Under the cover of naïveté, the language shows the awareness of the gulf that separated Hebraic faith from the cults of the world. Hebraic faith repudiated techniques for the possession of the Divine and tried only to place man at the disposal of the Ruler of history.

As the centuries wore on, belief in the " dwelling " of Yahweh on Mt. Zion lulled the Judeans into a false sense of security (Jer. 7:4-15). When the Babylonians razed their Temple (587 B.C.), however, they did not disintegrate. Decimated and uprooted, the " no-people " was the People of God still, for they had discovered a new mode of Presence. Yahweh was in their midst in a foreign land. Communion with the Divine had a universal quality.

IV

Hebraism became Judaism because the notion of People and the reality of Presence could never be separated from the proclamation of the *word* of Yahweh. Even in the old days, Presence was never meant to produce a feeling of mystical union, oblivious of social and political responsibility in history.

From the start, God had disclosed to his people a precise line of conduct: " Now, therefore, if ye will obey *my voice* indeed, and keep my covenant, then you shall be a peculiar treasure unto me " (Ex. 19:5).

The presence of God had always been articulate. Through Moses and the prophets, Yahweh *spoke* to his people:

> " *Hear,* O Israel, Yahweh thy God is an all-demanding Yahweh,
> and thou shalt love Yahweh thy God
> with all thy mind, all thy passion, and all thy life! "
>
> (Deut. 6:4-5.)

The early laws of the covenant (Ex. 20:21 to 23:21) and the later legislation of the Deuteronomic Code (Deut., chs. 12 to 26) sought to translate man's love to God into all the areas of life. It involved the engagement of man's total personality, without any divorce between individual and public integrity.

Israel, however, rejected the burden of the *word*. The stories of the Judges and of the Kings offer a monotonous sequence of apostasy and violence, " lingering perdition — worse than any death." The prophets of the eighth and seventh centuries b.c. enunciated Yahweh's *word* of warning, but in vain. Israel the bride had become a whore (Hos. 2:2; Ezek. 16:15). Revolt against the word had annulled the covenant (Jer. 31:32). Yet the prophets saw that the end of their political history would not terminate the life of the true Israel. Within the word of judgment, they heard a word of hope: " A remnant shall re-turn [better ' repent ']! " (Isa. 10:21). They envisioned a world where nature would be transformed, inequity would be eradi-cated, and an anointed child of David (Isa. 9:1-7; 11:1-9) would govern a purified people for the welfare of mankind.

The picture of a *remnant* led by a *messiah* (" anointed one "), together with the awareness of God's *presence* everywhere, as-sured the survival of the Jews in exile. At the direst hour of their death, they waited for the advent of the Kingdom of God.

In about 545 B.C., Second Isaiah told them the ringing *word* of comfort (Isa. 40:1-11). Israel was still the " slave " of Yahweh. Through her death and her resurrection, she would yet become " a light to the nations " (Isa. 42:6; 49:3; 52:13 to 53:12).

V

God's Kingdom was always " just around the corner," but it never came. The birth of Judaism may be ascribed to " delayed eschatology," since the Judeans became the Jews as they waited for the end (Greek *eschaton*) of history.

When Cyrus of Persia conquered Babylon in 539 B.C., freedom was granted to the ethnic minorities that had been deported there. Most of the Jews preferred to stay. Inspired by the universalism of Jeremiah, they had adapted themselves to life in a foreign land (Jer., ch. 29). Their descendants created the Judaism of the Diaspora (" dispersion "). Many emigrated to the various satrapies of the Persian empire (538–333 B.C.). Later, their sons moved to the Greek cities, to all the urban centers of the Hellenistic kingdoms (332–31 B.C.), and to the metropolitan centers of the Roman Empire. Through their synagogues Christianity spread in the Mediterranean world.

Other Jews in Babylon could not separate their faith from their worship of Yahweh on Mt. Zion. Influenced by the priestly program of Ezekiel (Ezek., chs. 40 to 48) and his disciples (Lev., chs. 17 to 26), they returned to Jerusalem and created the Palestinian Judaism of the second Temple (515 B.C. to A.D. 70). At first, they expected that Yahweh would soon inaugurate his reign under the " messiahship " of Zerubbabel (Hag. 2:22-23; Zech. 4:9), but their hope was not fulfilled.

In 397 B.C., the scribe Ezra imposed on the Jerusalem community a strict reform of ritual purity, to the point of enforcing the repudiation of foreign wives (Ezra 10:1-17; see Neh.

13:23-31). Palestinian Judaism became a closed sect, heroically clinging to the law. Passionate attachment to the Temple reached unparalleled devotion through the persecution of Antiochus Epiphanes (175–163 B.C.), the Maccabean wars (169–161 B.C.), and, a century later, the Roman rule of blood (67 B.C. to A.D. 70). More than ever in their history, the Jews of Palestine waited for the deliverance of Israel. It was in the midst of this final crisis that Jesus appeared, saying: " Love your enemies " (Matt. 5:44); " You are the light of the world " (Matt. 5:14; see Isa. 42:6).

VI

The Christian gospel sprang from a dynamic rethinking of the Hebraic sense of mission in history. The " royal priesthood " was reinterpreted in the context of Jeremiah's prediction of " a new covenant " (Jer. 31:31-33; see Heb. 8:8), and this reinterpretation once again presupposed the three cardinal elements of Hebraism: the *People,* the *Presence,* and the *Word.*

Like John the Baptist, the last of the prophets, Jesus preached the imminence of the Kingdom of God, but he added a new note: " The kingdom of God is at hand: Repent, and believe in the good news! " (Mark 1:15).

For him, the coming of the sovereign Judge of history was a source of awesome joy. By addressing himself to the poor (Isa. 61:1-3), and to such notorious outcasts as harlots and tax gatherers, he rediscovered the notion of " peoplehood " that had been at the root of Hebraism.

At the same time, Jesus related his concern for the people to his expectation of the end of history. Like most Jews of his time, he was possessed by eschatological fever, but he warned against the " apocalyptic " technique by which some tried to learn the exact date of the end of the age. When asked about the " signs of the time," he replied: " The kingdom of God is not coming with signs to be observed; nor will they say, ' Lo, here it is! ' or ' There! ' for behold, the kingdom of God is in the midst of you " (Luke 17:20-21). He likened that Kingdom to a mustard seed, or some leaven, and these parables suggest that, for him, the new world had to be prepared by the inner transformation of men. In some respects, Jesus did what Isaiah had done eight centuries earlier with his disciples (Isa. 8:16-18): he saw in them the seed of the remnant, the link between the two ages. In the new situation in which he lived, however, his notion of " People " exploded racial and ritual exclusivism.

At first, he ordered his disciples to preach the good news only to Jews: " Go nowhere among the Gentiles, and enter no town of the Samaritans, but go rather to the lost sheep of the house of Israel " (Matt. 10:5-6; see ch. 15:24). The faith of the Syrophoenician woman apparently took him by surprise (Matt. 15:28), and so did that of the Roman centurion at Capernaum (ch. 8:10). There is little doubt that he entertained a negative attitude toward Gentiles (Mark 7:24). But the opposition he encountered from the enlightened classes of his nation made him understand that some Jews would be cast out of the forthcoming community. He declared that many would come from the east and from the west and would sit down at the banquet with Abraham, Isaac, and Jacob. (Matt. 8:11.) In the parables of the marriage feast and of the husbandmen, he pictured the divine will to save all men, and he even implied the condemnation of the chosen race as a whole. The vineyard would be given to others. (Mark 12:9; Matt. 22:1-14.)

The internationalism and interracialism of the church was the outcome of the thought of Jesus himself. The early Christians went to " make disciples of all nations " (Matt. 28:19). Some of them, born Jews, wanted the newly converted pagans to become Jews as the initial step of their response to the gospel, and Peter himself wavered on this essential question (Gal.

2:11-14). Paul of Tarsus, however, formerly the proudest Jew of all (Rom. 11:1; Phil. 3:5), understood that in Christ all men are one. The church was the people of God, without privilege of sex, culture, class, race, color, or ritual (Gal. 3:28; Col. 3:11), bound together by the reality of Presence. From the slums of Corinth and of Rome, the villas of Antioch and of Damascus, the shops of Thessalonica and Athens, men and women of all walks of life — displaced persons, uprooted individuals, cultural and national orphans — who had been engulfed by the maelstrom of the Romans, suddenly found a home. And for the first time in the history of man, applied universalism was divorced from the imperialism of the weighted whip.

The church swept through hatred and estrangement. It was not another mystery cult or esoteric club, but the corporate company of those who felt " called " out of despair, and therefore " called upon " to manifest in their lives — and if necessary in their deaths — the presence of God, which they saw in the living Christ. The Presence, once again, created a People.

VII

The mystery of the person of Jesus remains unsolved through nineteen centuries of Christian thinking and ten generations of historical research. Little is known about his origins, his infancy, his adolescence, his intellectual and spiritual formation. But the early Christian remembered him as the Christ.

The early Christians remembered him as the Christ, but not in the sense of a political " messiah," who would deliver the Jews from the yoke of Rome with swords and legions of angels on the last day. They told how he had rejected the lure of material power, of egocentric desire, of mystical identification with infinity (Matt. 4:1-11; Luke 4:1-13). They knew that he looked at himself not at all by the mirror of political messianism (he refused to be crowned king) but through the image of one "anointed" to preach good tidings to the meek and to bind up the brokenhearted (Isa. 61:1-3; see Luke 4:17-19). Symbols of military glitter would have been for him ludicrous and irrelevant, because his whole power of being radiated the holy. He spoke of himself as "the son of man," but they saw in him far more than the epitome of manhood. They called him "the son of God." He reflected for them nothing less than the enormous presence of Divinity.

Let us observe the pattern in which the Christian memory of Jesus was molded. It represents a reinterpretation of the Hebraic theology of Presence. Mark opens his Gospel with words from Malachi. (Mark 1:2; Mal. 3:1.)

At the heart of the ministry, the Evangelists depict the scene of the transfiguration. Three disciples have a vision of Moses and Elijah (the Law and the Prophets), standing together with the radiant figure. "And his raiment became shining, exceeding white as snow, . . . and there was a cloud that overshadowed them." (Mark 9:2-8; see Matt. 17:1-8; Luke 9:28-36.) We recognize here the "thick darkness," which signals the presence of God on Mt. Sinai and his "sojourning" in the Temple. And during the trial of Jesus, witnesses deposed that he had said: "I will destroy this temple that is made with hands, and in three days I will build another, not made with hands" (Mark 14:58). The risen Christ had become for the early Christians the new temple of God. They had by him access to the Holy of Holies. The veil had been rent in two (Mark 15:38), and they moved about the world, energized by the commission couched in the words of the old Hebraic visions of God: "Lo, I am with you always, to the close of the age" (Matt. 28:20).

The church came into being as the shrine of that Presence, and Paul could write even to the wretched Corinthians, who surely did not pass for models of heroism or morality, "We are the temple of the living God" (II Cor. 6:16). He broke

open the exclusiveness of priestly Judaism (quoting Ezek.
37:27; Ex. 29:45; Lev. 26:12). In the sacrament of the Word,
the Presence was enshrined no longer in the space of Zion but
in the time of the Eucharist (I Cor. 11:26).

The church was the People in whom the presence of God
was made manifest. When those tentmakers and shopkeepers
broke the bread and drank the wine in common, their act was
not done in memory of a dead philosopher or of a gentle seer
whose words had for a while brought a glimmer of optimism to
a world of violent death. No, they were communing with a
very present God, and far more important still, they were hail-
ing his tomorrow. The cup of the new covenant (I Cor. 11:25)
was for them the sign and warrant of his final triumph (v. 26)
and of their commitment.

If we say that Judaism was born from delayed eschatology,
we may add that the church was an incarnate eschatology. That
is to say, the early Christians formed in their flesh (*in carne*),
here on earth, the living body of the Christ in the age to come.
The People of the Presence, in the face of their apparent mortality, proclaimed the eternal Word.

VIII

Always the three cardinal elements: the People, the Presence,
and the Word. It is thrilling to discern how, in various ways,
and with diverse expressions of language, the church sought to
formulate for herself and for her converts the newness of her
faith. She did it by rethinking the formulations of her Hebraic
heritage, largely ignoring the Judaism of her time.

For example, The Gospel According to Luke attempted
to convey the marvel of the coming into human history of
Jesus, born of a woman, and yet so different from other sons
of men. Therefore, he prefaced the story of the birth of Jesus
with the " annunciation," one of the most profound theologi-

cal meditations on the meaning of Christ. " The power of the Most High shall *overshadow* thee." (Luke 1:35.) Again we hear the word of the sojourning Presence, the thick darkness of Mt. Sinai, the Temple, and the transfiguration.

A different approach is made toward the end of the first century A.D. by another theologian of the mystery of Christ: " In the beginning was the Word, . . . and the Word was made flesh and *sojourned* among us, . . . full of grace and truth " (John 1:1, 14). Once again, we hear the Word of the sojourning Presence, alighting as in a tent, only for a night. The Hebraic theology of the Temple reappears. This time, however, the language introduces us to the motif of " the Word made flesh." The divine Word is made a man. Mortal manhood, on the planet earth, is inhabited by a divine reality.

We are now able to turn to the second part of our inquiry. Why and how were these things written? (John 20:31.) How can the Bible be called, with intellectual honesty, " the Word of God "?

CHAPTER 2 | *The Birth of the Book*

THE Word was spoken and acted before it was written. Let us attempt to go beyond the familiar expression " the Word of God " and to inquire into its origin.

In Hebrew, the term *dabhar,* " word," meant a proposition spoken in solemn circumstances, which was endowed with an objective, almost independent quality. It could hardly be distinguished from the decision, act, or event that it sought to portray. Particularly when it was used for God (more than 400 times in the Bible), such a term suggested an intermediary agent between the infinity of the divine and the finiteness of the human. For example, the Hebrews said it was through his Word that God created heaven and earth (Gen., ch. 1; see Ps. 147:15-18; etc.). The prophets described the peculiarity of their experiences by repeating again and again: " The word of Yahweh came to me " (Jer. 1:4; etc.), or even: " the words . . . which [I] saw . . ." (Amos 1:1; etc.). The Word of God is a dynamic reality that creates and re-creates, and it " will stand for ever " (Isa. 40:8). It does not return to him " void " or " empty," but it accomplishes what he wills. (Isa. 55:11.) We can now understand why the Bible has been called " the Word of God." Its words become the mediators of God's life among men because they tell of his action and picture the way in which he promotes events in our history. Therefore, to depict God's act of supreme purpose, the church proclaimed: " The Word was made flesh " (John 1:1, 14).

If the Word is God's creative and dynamic intervention among men, selecting the method of utter weakness, with suffering and death upon a cross (at the hands of men!), the Christian reader will know at once that the Bible participates in limitations of several kinds, such as formulation in human thought and language. The world views of writers who labored two or three thousand years ago in some remote corner of the Mediterranean become merely the elements of historical relativity. To speak of inerrancy in the words of Scripture is to misunderstand completely the very method of communication that God used in order to disclose himself to men.

The miracle of the Bible lies not in its writing but in its ability to transmit to men of every age the absolute rigor of God's love. We are free in our commitment to that absolute love to investigate this library with the utmost honesty of intellect. To love God with all our mind creates in us the solemn duty to search and to understand the universe, his creation, and also the Bible, which is the record of his intervention.

I

Analysis of the Bible has shown to modern man that the idea of a " Holy Scripture " was the result of a complex and slow process. The ancient Hebrews were not historians and memorialists in the modern sense of the terms, bent upon putting down in writing the events of their times. Their concern was not what is now called the art of biography or the science of historiography, but they worshiped their God at certain places and at certain seasons of the year. And the ceremonies which they celebrated, as they constituted a People assembled in the Presence, always included the recital of a Word. They dramatically rehearsed the acts of God. The cult was the matrix of what became many centuries later " the Bible."

At Passover, in early spring; at Weeks (Pentecost), in early summer; and at Tabernacles (Booths), in early autumn, the ancient Hebrews gathered in order " to seek the face of Yahweh." Their first " literature " was born then and there, through dance and song, in joy and enthusiasm. Accompanied by wind, string, and percussion instruments, singers chanted liturgically of the oaks of Mamre, where Abraham their father had met the mysterious envoys, renewing his vision of a posterity for the peace of all men; of the Moriah hill, where he had endured the ordeal of giving up his son and his hopes; of the canyon of Jabbok, where Jacob (" the heel-kicker "), afraid and alone amid the oleanders, had fought until the break of dawn and received a new name, " Israel," or " God will prevail."

When Joshua formed at Shechem the twelve-tribe confederacy (about 1230 B.C.), the Hebrews renewed covenant with their God (Josh., ch. 24), the covenant that Moses had initiated in the name of Yahweh with the Joseph clans after the exodus from Egypt. There, the whole nation was told again of the deeds, the promises, the summonses, the warnings, and always the tireless love of their God. Each season, each year, each century, the epic of their peculiar past, token of their unique mission, received a " literary " shape, although still unwritten.

Oral traditions that now form the basis of Genesis, Exodus, Numbers, Leviticus, Deuteronomy, Joshua, and Judges were originally cultic recitals of faith. The worshipers rehearsed them as creeds in narrative form (see, for example, Deut. 26:5-10).

Such a creed, and other liturgical pieces like it, formed the nucleus of the written Bible. With their changes of pronouns, they bring the past into the cultic present.

II

During the reign of David or soon thereafter (tenth century B.C.), an unknown prophet, perhaps Nathan, perhaps another, collected the poems and the stories together and published them as the first " catechism " of the nation. He may have used several earlier books as well as oral traditions, for we know that such documents, now lost, existed in his days (for example, " the Book of the Righteous," Josh. 10:12-13; " the Book of the Wars of Yahweh," Num. 21:14). However, his purpose was not just to preserve " old, unhappy, far-off things, and battles long ago."

He wanted to prepare the future by looking at history as an organic stage, where the Creator of the universe watches over man and seeks to heal man's folly. This unknown man conceived the idea of " history " as the " story " of God's grand design for the healing of the nations. The editor of this earliest catechism has been called " the Yahwist " because he used the name " Yahweh " for the God of the patriarchs before the time of Moses (Ex. 3:15), and this designation is often abbreviated as " J " (from the German spelling " Jahveh "). Long before the Greeks, Augustine, Bossuet, Spengler, or Toynbee, the Yahwist proposed a worldwide interpretation of the human epic, but he did so in order to warn his nation against the illusions of nationalism and to remind her of her priestly mission.

After the disruption of Solomon's kingdom (922 B.C.), a similar collection was made in Northern Israel from the point of view not of Judah but of the Joseph tribes (Ephraim). Strands of this collection were uncovered in Genesis, Exodus, and Deuteronomy (hence, the duplication of many stories therein), and have been ascribed to an unknown prophet of the north whom scholars have designated as " the Elohist " because he called God " Elohim " before the revelation of the name " Yahweh " to Moses (Ex. 3:14-15). This designation is abbreviated as " E." There is, however, some doubt whether these northern " traditions " were ever published as an independent " body " similar to that of " J."

As conditions of existence were transformed, and the sons of the Hebrew nomads became farmers, industrialists, and international tradesmen, the ancient laws of the covenant needed to be adapted to a new cultural situation. Indeed, legislation in the civil, criminal, and cultic realms was constantly amplified throughout the centuries of the Judges, Samuel, Saul, David, Solomon, especially Omri and Ahab (1200–850 B.C.).

Such laws formed the core of the Deuteronomic Code (or " D," chiefly in Deut., chs. 12 to 26), which was preserved after the fall of Israel (722 B.C.) at the Temple of Jerusalem in Judah. It was in all probability the D Code that was found there a century later by the servants of King Josiah and that inspired his reform (621 B.C.). The D Code incorporated in terms of practical legislation a high ideal of clean worship, integrity of character, and fairness in public morality. It was this book which gave to the Judeans, and later the Jews, the idea of a sacred " Scripture." The written " Word " was slowly gaining authority for the life and faith of succeeding generations.

During the Babylonian exile (587–538 B.C.), the sons of the Jerusalem priests were inspired both by Deuteronomy and by Ezekiel, chs. 40 to 48, to prepare a restoration by writing down their memories of cultic ceremonial and of social ethics which they had received from their ancestors. In due course, the priestly laws and narratives (or " P ") were woven together with the earlier strands, J, E, and D, in an effort to maintain intact the entire treasure of the nation's heritage.

Thus, the fruit of five or six centuries of literary labor came to its maturity. It was called " the Law," for it became the charter of worship and morals in the second Temple, where it was probably read for the first time by Ezra in 397 B.C. As the scribes preserved it on five scrolls kept in five amphorae (in Greek, *penta teukhea*), later Jews called it " Pentateuch."

Knowledge of the origins and growth of the Pentateuch suggests that extreme caution be exercised in its interpretation. We must be prepared to find in it primitive and bloody stories (as in Ex. 4:24) side by side with the lofty command to love one's neighbor (Lev. 19:18). At the same time, when the various traditions are placed in the specific situations of history that brought them to birth, the very stuff of divine pathos and of human striving emerges from the yarns.

III

The prophets of the eighth century and their successors were the troubadours of Yahweh's love in a doomed nation. While they failed to save Israel or Judah from political extermination, their poems were committed to memory by their disciples and edited at a later time in the books that now bear their names.

The term " literary prophets " is misleading, for the books were written long after the prophets had lived. This is demonstrated by the style and language of titles and superscriptions, the contents and arrangement of the material, and many other details of internal analysis.

Another error arises from the traditional titles " Major Prophets " (Isaiah, Jeremiah, and Ezekiel; Daniel is not listed as a prophet in the Hebrew manuscripts) and " Minor Prophets " (the Twelve). Such titles refer to the relative *length* of the books, not to the importance of the prophets themselves.

Finally, the order in which the books appear in the Old Testament does not correspond to the chronological sequence of the prophets. Here again, the word sprang from the midst of history. We must read the prophetic poems in their concrete contexts. We must think of Amos, Hosea, First Isaiah (chs.

1 to 39), and Micah in the eighth century; Jeremiah, Zephaniah, Nahum, and Habakkuk in the seventh; Ezekiel, Second Isaiah (chs. 40 to 55), Haggai, and Zechariah in the sixth; probably Joel, Jonah, and Malachi in the fifth.

While some of the prophets' words are couched in the style of casual speech, most of their utterances constitute " poetry " in the strict and formal sense of the term. They follow rhythmic and poetic patterns that represent a long tradition of refinement and craftsmanship. Thought is married to form according to laws of lyrical, epic, satirical, or elegiac elocution. Methods of interpretation clearly depend on literary and historical analysis. The perenniality of the word, in the books of the prophets as in the books of the law, will grasp the reader even while he listens to the hustle of circumstantial events.

Some of the prophetic books are anthologies covering three or more centuries. The " book " of Isaiah, for instance, includes not only the sayings of the eighth-century prophet (chiefly in chs. 1 to 12 and 28 to 32) but also other pieces, long or short, such as the monument of " Second Isaiah " (chs. 40 to 55; sixth century B.C.), the oracles and prayers in chs. 56 to 66, and the hymns of chs. 24 to 27.

The books of the Three and of the Twelve are designated in the Hebrew manuscripts as the " Latter Prophets," for they are preceded by the books of Joshua, Judges, Samuel, and Kings, which are known as the " Former Prophets." In many ways, this traditional Jewish name is better than the Christian designation, " Historical Books," because these books represent a " prophetic " interpretation of the nation's history from its conquest of the land to its expulsion from it.

It is important to remember that, while the Pentateuch in its present form was completed before the collections of the Prophets, the bulk of the writings in both bodies grew simultaneously. Both were edited chiefly during and after the Babylonian exile (sixth century B.C.). In both cases, literary activity was induced by the threat of national death. The Bible was born from historical agony.

IV

A similar complexity may be seen at the birth of the "Poetic Books" (Job, Psalms, Proverbs), the five "Festive Scrolls" (still sung at the five festivals of Judaism: Song of Songs, Lamentations, Ruth, Ecclesiastes, Esther), and the postexilic "Writings" (Chronicles, Ezra-Nehemiah, Daniel).

The making of almost each one of these books represents the work of several generations. The Psalter was the hymnal of the second Temple, but it includes hymns and prayers of many centuries, from Ps. 29 ("The seven thunders"), earlier than David, to Ps. 137 ("By the rivers of Babylon") and Ps. 126 ("When the Lord restored the captivity of Zion"). The *poem* of Job (chs. 3 to 31; 38 to 42:6) was probably composed during the exile, but the *folktale* which forms its setting and occasion (chs. 1 and 2; 42:7-17) goes back orally to the time of David or earlier. The collection of Proverbs includes maxims from Solomon's diplomats, the translated sentences of an old Egyptian wise man called Amen-em-opet, as well as the reflections of Jewish teachers of wisdom in Persian Jerusalem (fifth century B.C.). The extraordinarily keen story of Ruth told the contemporaries of the racially minded Ezra (fifth to fourth century) that David's grandmother, after all, was a foreign woman, but it was based on memories of early times (1100 B.C.). The editor of Chronicles revised for the benefit of the Temple musicians in Persian days the books of Judges, Samuel, and Kings, but he made use of ancient archives apparently unknown to his predecessors. Even the latest book of the Old Testament, the apocalypse of Daniel, composed and published in the white heat of end-of-the-world fever

THE BIRTH OF THE HEBREW BIBLE

Historical Dates B.C.	I. The Law	II. The Prophets — 1. Former Prophets	II. The Prophets — 2. Latter Prophets	1. wisdom poetry	III. The Hagiographa — 2. lyric poetry	III. The Hagiographa — 3. prose
Patriarchs ....ca. 1800	tribal sagas					oral traditions
Exodus ....ca. 1275	ballads	oral traditions		folktale	cultic	Temple archives
Conquest ....ca. 1230	oral epics	memoirs		maxims	songs	genealogies
Monarchy ....ca. 1000	oral laws → J	archives, oral cycles of Elijah-Elisha				
Schism 922	E		Amos, Hosea			
Fall of Israel 722	D		I Isaiah, Micah			
Fall of Judah, Exile in Babylon ..587	P → Pentateuch	Kings, Samuel Judges, Joshua	Jeremiah, Zephaniah Nahum, Habakkuk	Job	Lamentations	
End of Exile 538			Ezekiel, II Isaiah		Song of Songs	Ruth
Second Temple 515			Haggai, Zechariah, 1-8 Joel, Malachi Isaiah, 56-66 Zechariah, 9-14 Isaiah, 24-27		Psalms	
Nehemiah 444						
Ezra 397			Jonah	Proverbs		Chronicles Ezra, Nehemiah
Maccabeans 168						Ecclesiastes Esther, Daniel

at the climactic moment of the Maccabean wars (165–164 B.C.), preserved earlier narratives of the sixth and fifth centuries B.C.

These books appear at the end of the Hebrew Bible, after the Pentateuch and the Prophets, and they are called the " Holy Writings," or " Hagiographa " (from the Greek, *ta hagia grapha*). When the growth of the Old Testament is viewed as a whole, one fact emerges: the three distinct bodies of this literature — Law, Prophets, and Hagiographa — were formed side by side together over long sequences of time, but the literary urge that created the bulk of the thirty-nine books of the Hebrew Bible reached its peak during the cultural crisis of the sixth century B.C. Most of them represent the attempt of a people, at the brink of extinction, to salvage from " the dark backward and abysm of time " the voice of a God who does not die with the crashes of empires. By the written echo of the Word, a remnant of sons could still live and rebuild.

V

During the Hellenistic and Roman times (fourth century B.C. to first century A.D.), the Jews of Palestine as well as the Jews of the Diaspora (especially in Alexandria), wrote a great many books, secular as well as religious. Several of these were adopted as sacred by the Greek-speaking synagogues of the Roman Empire, but not by Palestinian Jewry. They were called " Apocrypha " (" hidden away ") by some of the early Christians (see Chapter 3, and Lawrence E. Toombs, *The Threshold of Christianity,* in this series).

Other religious writings of the period have come down to us. Because the fashion was for an author to ascribe a new book to a great figure of the past, many of these documents are known as the " Pseudepigrapha," some of the most influential of which were apocalypses written in the pattern of Daniel.

THE LITERATURE OF JUDAISM
IN HELLENISTIC AND ROMAN TIMES

Historical Dates	I. The Apocrypha	II. The Pseudepigrapha	III. Others
B.C. Ptolemaic rule (Alexandria)			Story of Ahiqar
321	Tobit		
Seleucid rule (Antioch) .198	Additions to Esther Ecclesiasticus (Sirach) I Baruch Judith Song of the 3 Children	Testaments of XII Patriarchs	
Hasmonaean kings 161	I Esdras (III Ezra) I Maccabees II Maccabees	I Enoch (Ethiopic Enoch) Jubilees Zadokite Fragment Sibylline Oracles (III)	Manual of Discipline (Qumrân) Wars of Sons of Light and Darkness (Qumrân) Hymns (Qumrân)
	Susanna	Epistle of Jeremy	Commentary on Hab., chs. 1, 2 (Qumrân)
Roman rule ...63	Bel and the Dragon Wisdom of Solomon	Letter of Aristeas Psalms of Solomon	
Herod the Great. 40			
Birth of Jesus ca. 6 Procurators 4		III Maccabees IV Maccabees Prayer of Manasses	The Lives of the Prophets
Christian era			
Death of Jesus ca. 30		Assumption of Moses Martyrdom of Isaiah Paralipomena of Jeremiah Life of Adam and Eve (Apocalypse of Moses) II Baruch (Syriac Baruch) II Enoch (Slavonic Enoch, or The Secrets of Enoch)	Philosophical Works of Philo of Alexandria (d. A.D. 42)
Jewish revolt ..66 Destruction of Jerusalem ..70		II Esdras (IV Ezra) Sayings of the Fathers (Pirke Aboth)	
Revolt of Bar Kocheba ..135		Apocalypse of Abraham III Baruch (Greek Baruch)	Historical works of Flavius Josephus (d. ca. A.D. 105)

It is of extreme importance for the student of early Christianity to know " the best sellers " in the time of Jesus.

VI

The birth of the Christian literature is quite similar to that of the Pentateuch and the Prophets. The Gospels, on the one hand, represent the catechism and preaching of the early church, when the acts of Christ were liturgically recited. Just as Passover became the Christian Easter, so, also, Christians celebrated their liberation from mortal existence by reciting the " Word-Deed " of Christ, author of their " exodus."

The epistles, on the other hand, which had been occasional notes or letters written chiefly by Paul to various communities, soon were copied, read, and collected as the " prophetic word " of the apostles of Christ to the church. Incidentally, the epistles are also similar to the books of Amos or Jeremiah in one other respect: they preserve the actual words of the preachers of the Lord, and they become in their turn the seed of a perennial " word " of God in a new historical situation.

The rise of the gospel tradition is comparable to the growth of the exodus and covenant narratives in the ancient Hebrew sanctuaries. Gathered in the presence of the living Christ, the men and women of Pentecost recited in unison, with prayer, hymns, and the celebration of the Lord's Supper, the words that Jesus had spoken and the stories that they had witnessed or in which they had taken part. The cultic act was the setting, once again, of " literary " formulation. Indeed, Christ was speaking still. The Presence linked the words of memory with the Word of continual self-disclosure. The Presence was the catalyst of memory in the pitch of expectation. As for the people of the old covenant, the people of the new covenant, in their drama of worship, recited the words of their past, but their waiting for their imminent future transmuted these

THE GROWTH OF THE LITERATURE OF THE NEW COVENANT

World History A.D.	Christian History A.D.	Gospels & The Acts	Epistles
Tiberius 14			
Pontius Pilate, procurator 26	John the Baptist 26		
	Jesus in Galilee 29		
	Jesus in Jerusalem ..30	Gospel traditions	
	Church in Judea 31		
	Church in Syria 32		
	Conversion of Paul ...33		
Caligula 37			
Claudius 41			
	Church in Asia Minor..45		
Famine in Palestine 46	Council of Jerusalem ..46		
	Paul's rebuke of Peter at Antioch ...48	L Q M	
Jews' expulsion from Rome 49	Church in Europe 49		
	Paul in Corinth 50		I Thess. II Thess.
Gallio, proconsul of Achaia 51			
Felix, procurator ...52	Paul at Ephesus 52		I Cor. Gal.
Nero 54			II Cor. Rom.
	Paul in Macedonia ...55		
	Paul in Jerusalem 56		
	Paul in Caesarea 57		
Festus, procurator ..58	Paul in Rome 59		Col. Philem.
	Persecution in Rome ..64		Phil.
		Mark	
Jewish Revolt 66	Flight of Jerusalem church to Pella 66		James
Galba, Otho, Vitellius .69			
Vespasian 69			
Fall of Jerusalem ...70		Luke Matt. Acts	
Titus 79		John	Heb.
Domitian 81			Eph. I, II, Tim. Titus
	Persecution in Rome ..95		Rev. I Pet.
Nerva 96			I, II, III John
Trajan 98			Jude
	Pliny's Repression ..112		
	Death of Ignatius ...115		II Pet.

words into a present Word. *The Lord is coming!* Such was the motivation of the fever which seized the early church at worship. The hope of his return in glory spurred the articulation of their memory. They anticipated their tomorrow by bringing their past into their cultic present.

The account of the passion and death of Jesus became the nucleus of the gospel tradition (see Acts 2:23; 4:27; I Cor. 2:2; 11:23-27). There was at first no need to write "lives of Jesus," for the early church expected the end of the world at any moment. The "literary-oral" phase of the Gospel material resulted from delayed eschatology.

When the eyewitnesses died, one after another, popular imagination had already begun to embroider the story. It was imperative for the Christian leaders of the second generation to put in writing the memories of the early disciples (see "preface" of The Gospel According to Luke, ch. 1:1-4).

The Gospels of Matthew, Mark, and Luke form a group apart from the Fourth Gospel, for they contain much of the same material (not unlike the J and E traditions in the Pentateuch). Their similarities are such that one can arrange them side by side on three parallel columns in order to facilitate comparison at one glance. The first three Gospels are called "Synoptics," from the Greek, *syn-opsis,* "view together."

For many centuries, scholars have tried to explain the origin of the Synoptics in such a way as to account for both their common characteristics and their distinctive features. Thanks to the minute investigation of many, like Johann Wettstein (1730), J. A. Bengel (1742), John Wesley (1755), F. C. Baur (1847), Johannes Weiss (1892), W. Bousset (1892), M. Dibelius (1919), R. Bultmann (1921), V. Taylor (1933), it appears that the Gospel of Mark, the earliest of the three, was not written before the time of Nero's persecution of the Christians of Rome (A.D. 64). Matthew and Luke probably came out as revised and augmented, although independent, editions of Mark, between A.D. 75 and 85.

VII

The author of the earliest Gospel, Mark, may have been " the youth wearing a linen cloth " who witnessed the arrest of Jesus and fled naked (Mark 14:51-52 only). He was possibly the same as John Mark (Acts 12:12), who was associated with the apostles at an early date (Acts 12:25; 13:5, 13; 15:36-39), and may have been at a later date the assistant of Peter and Paul in Rome (II Tim. 4:11; I Peter 5:13). Eusebius, in the fourth century, reports that, according to Papias, a second-century "*episkopos*": " Mark, having become the interpreter of Peter, wrote down accurately all that he remembered of the things done and said by Christ." Alone among the Evangelists, Mark has preserved concrete details, such as the grieved glance of Jesus (Mark 3:5), the pillow on which he slept through the storm (ch. 4:38), the green grass on which the crowd sat " like banquet guests," in rows " like garden beds " (ch. 6:39-40). He also respected the Aramaic language in which Jesus addressed the daughter of Jairus (ch. 5:41) or the deaf man (ch. 7:34), as if to retain the vocal inflection, which was perhaps still ringing in the aged ears of Peter.

Both authors of the Gospels of Matthew and Luke used and edited the Gospel of Mark, either in its present form or in a preliminary draft, now lost (" Proto-Mark "). In addition, they had access to a collection of the "Words" (*Logia*) of Jesus, which scholars have called " Q," from the German " *Quelle*" (" [common] source "), which must have existed for several years in a fairly fixed form (discourses, and parables common to Matthew and Luke). Finally, the same authors independently had access to separate and specific traditions, which have been called respectively " L " and " M."

The Gospel of Matthew reflects the memories of the tax col-
lector Levi, called Matthew (Matt. 9:9 only; see Mark 2:14;
Luke 5:27), who apparently moved at a later date to the Jewish-Christian community in Antioch. His work is divided into
five parts, like the five scrolls of the Pentateuch. With ample
quotations from the Old Testament, "Matthew" clearly attempts to present "the law" of the New Age.

VIII

The Gospel of "Luke," on the contrary, reflects the theology
of pagan Christians. Its author was a cultured man who wrote
excellent Greek and was conscious of historiographical methods (Luke 3:1, 23; etc.). He probably had received some information from the direct family of Jesus through none other
than Luke, "the beloved physician," companion of Paul's
travels (Acts 21:8, 17; see Col. 4:14).

The Lucan editor and writer incorporated in his work a
large bulk of material that was almost totally unknown to
Matthew (Luke 9:49 to 18:30), and he also differed sig-
nificantly from both Mark and Matthew in his accounts of the
Nativity and of the Passion. He used a genealogy that presented Jesus not only as the son of David and Abraham but
also as the son of Adam (Luke 3:24-38). Whereas in Matthew, astrologers asked for the "king of the Jews" (Matt.
2:2), in Luke, Simeon sang a hymn of hope for all nations
(Luke 2:29-35). The Lucan writer included stories on the Samaritans, whom Jews abhorred (chs. 10:25-37; 17:11-19); he
showed interest for despised classes (chs. 18:9-14; 19:1-10) and
the poor (chs. 2:7, 10; 3:11; 4:18; 6:20, 24; 12:16-21; 16:19-31);
he was delighted by Jesus' kindness to women and children
(chs. 7:36-50; 8:2-3; 10:38-42; 11:27; 23:27-28). He did not refrain from revealing the emotions of a human Jesus (chs.
19:41-44; 22:44). He insisted on the teaching of Jesus about

prayer (chs. 11:5-9; 18:1, 7, 9-14); above all, he pictured Jesus praying (chs. 3:21; 5:16; 6:12; etc.).

Far from stressing, as Matthew did, the Jewishness of Jesus and the eschatological aspect of his teaching (see Matt. 1:1-17; 10:5; 23:2; ch. 25; etc.), he emphasized salvation for all men and in this age (Luke 19:11), for he pictured the virtue of grace that rescues even existence from the vicissitudes of the present. At the same time, there is no trace of anti-Judaism in his work (as there seems to be in the Fourth Gospel). Above all, he included the poetry of exquisite Hebraic diction that formed the first treasury of Christian hymnody, and still stands at the heart of the liturgy: the Magnificat, the Benedictus, the Ave Maria, the Gloria in Excelsis Deo, and the Nunc Dimittis. And it is in Luke alone that the literary and theological diamonds of the gospel are found: the parables of the lost sheep, of the lost coin, of the elder brother, and of the good Samaritan. No wonder that in the Middle Ages "Luke" became the patron saint of music and the arts.

The Acts of the Apostles forms the sequence of the Lucan Gospel (compare the preface of Luke 1:1-4 with that of Acts 1:1-4). The author wished to inform a certain Theophilus, probably a Roman official, of the origins of Christian faith, either to convert or to enlighten him. The book traces the march of faith from Jerusalem to Rome, and it seeks to stress the unity of the church, already rent by dissension (compare the account of the first council of Jerusalem, A.D. 46, in Acts, ch. 15, with the testimony of Paul in Gal. 2:11-14). The use of the early sermons of Peter and Stephen is of great historical significance (Acts, chs. 2 to 7), and so is that of a travel diary, probably kept by Luke, the physician (the "We" source in chs. 16:10-18; 20:5-16; 21:1-18; 27:1 to 28:16). Without the book of The Acts, we should know next to nothing about the early days of Christianity and the travels of Paul.

IX

The Synoptic Gospels and The Acts dealt with the events that brought forth the new faith, but they did not represent the birth of Christian literature. They came at a time when most of the letters of Paul had already been written and collected.

Paul undertook his first missionary journey with a colorful Cypriot, Barnabas (Acts 4:36), the uncle of John Mark, who had introduced the newly converted Pharisee to the suspicious apostles (ch. 9:27), and had trained him to preach (ch. 11:22-26). After a year of collaboration in Antioch, Barnabas and Saul spread the church to Cyprus and Galatia in central Asia Minor (chs. 13 and 14; about A.D. 45). The problem created by the influx of uncircumcised pagans into the church was amicably settled at the council of Jerusalem (Acts, ch. 15; A.D. 46). Christianity was emancipated from legalism.

After the council of Jerusalem, Paul returned alone to the Galatian churches and brought the gospel to Europe (Acts, chs. 16 to 18; A.D. 49), in Philippi, Thessalonica, Athens, and especially the large commerce and sports center of Corinth. It was there that he received disturbing news of the newly Christianized Thessalonians. Some of them had died, and the question arose: Would the dead then be excluded from the Kingdom of God when the Lord Christ returns? Paul wrote to give them reassurance. His first letter to the Thessalonians was to be the first literary document of the New Testament (A.D. 50).

A few months later, some Christians of Salonica had stopped working, so eager were they for the coming of the New Age. Paul wrote to them to instill some " good sense " into their irresponsibility. This note was eventually to be known as II Thessalonians (A.D. 51).

Again, the principle of literary creation is due to delayed eschatology. The motivation for the writing of the first documents of the Christian literature was the need "to temper the madness of long-frustrated hopes." Thanks to the realism of Paul, who understood "the mind of Christ," the church learned to live for the Kingdom to come, and to work as if it had already come! Hoping for heaven, Christians planted their feet on the ground.

Having returned to Jerusalem from Corinth (A.D. 52), Paul spent some time at Antioch and undertook a third missionary journey through Asia Minor. He remained two or three years at Ephesus, the metropolis of the west coast. It was there that he "fought against lions," whether literally or not, and wrote some of his major letters, one to the Galatians and the first two of his four to the Corinthians.

A "fundamentalist" party of Jewish-Christian origin had undermined in Paul's absence the freedom of the gospel in Galatia. He wrote to the Galatians in an outburst of passion, spelling out the mystery of crucifixion with Christ. He showed that obedience to ritual was still a manifestation of pride, since the man who fulfills the law remains in a sense the master of his destiny. The letter to the Galatians has been called the Magna Charta of Christianity.

From Ephesus also, Paul heard that the Christians of Corinth were in discord on matters of faith and of behavior. He wrote them a first letter, now lost (I Cor. 5:9).

A second letter has survived: it is now called I Corinthians, also written from Ephesus in the spring of A.D. 55 (see I Cor. 16:8-9). A third letter followed, written from Macedonia in A.D. 56, after a second visit to Corinth (see II Cor. 12:14; 13:1-2; Acts 20:2). By mistaken editing, it has been preserved as chs. 10 to 16 of II Corinthians. Allusions to this third letter are found in II Cor. 2:3, 4; 7:8-12. It was a note of rebuke, in which the apostle bared his heart. In order to show to the Corinthians that his opponents were only "pseudo apostles"

(II Cor. 11:13), in spite of their blood, Paul had to boast about himself. He felt humiliated by this boasting, but he went to excesses of language in order to regain the confidence of his deceived friends. He even wrote of the ecstasies that had ravished him (II Cor. 11:2 to 13:13). It is a rare document, which provides a link in the unpremeditated literature of spirituality between the confessions of Jeremiah and the cries of the medieval saints. Finally, a few weeks afterward, again from Macedonia (A.D. 56), Paul wrote a fourth note of reconciliation, now preserved in chs. 1 to 9 of II Corinthians.

The letter to the Romans was composed at the same time, also from Macedonia, while Paul planned to go to Rome and Spain (Acts 19:21; Rom. 1:11; 15:23-24), and was compelled to postpone his visit. Fearing that the faith of the Roman community, already " famous in the entire world " (Rom. 1:8), was being given a Jewish twist similar to that inflicted upon the Galatians, he addressed the Christians of Rome formally in order to expound the Christian principle of life and faith in the individual (chs. 1 to 8), in history (chs. 9 to 11), and in the church (chs. 12 to 15). An appendix, accidentally attached to the earlier manuscripts of Romans, belongs to a lost letter probably addressed to the Ephesians (ch. 16). The Letter of Paul to the Romans became the heart of Christian theology.

Ignoring the advice of friends, the fighting evangelist returned to Jerusalem (A.D. 56), possessed by the zeal to preach there at all cost (Acts, ch. 21). He was promptly arrested, and spent the rest of his life known to us either in jail — chiefly in Caesarea — or in enforced residence in Rome. He may have died there during the persecution of Nero (A.D. 64). At any rate, it was in Rome that he probably wrote, between the years 60 and 62, the letter to the Philippians, chiefly on the mystery of the Christ (Phil. 2:6-11).

In his short letter to Philemon, of Colossae in Phrygia, Paul recommended welcome to Onesimus, a slave who had run away and who was now willingly returning to his master. The letter to the Colossians was also written from Rome at that time (A.D. 63-64), as well as a circular letter perhaps originally addressed to the Laodiceans, now preserved as The Letter of Paul to the Ephesians. The apostle pleaded for the unity of the church, the bride of Christ (Col. 1:18).

X

After the fall of Jerusalem in A.D. 70, Christianity was truly detached from the Temple ritual. On the one hand, The Letter to the Hebrews, composed by a disciple of Paul, sought to describe the Christ as the true High Priest, Sacrificial Victim, and Sanctuary of the new covenant. The Letter of James, on the other hand, also written to Christians of Jewish origin, misunderstood the reality of faith (which for Paul involved total surrender) as a merely intellectual belief (ch. 5:19), and insisted on the necessity of good works. In spite of its deficiencies, it saw the dangers of " antinomianism " (lawlessness).

The First Letter of Peter may come from the apostle Peter, if one supposes that the Galilean fisherman did not perish in the persecution of Nero in A.D. 64, lived to an advanced age, and learned to write in a literary Greek style. It is more likely to have grown from Peter's entourage, toward the end of the first century. The letters of Jude and especially II Peter reflect the ideas and institutions of a later time.

XI

The books that are attached to the name of John are varied in style and contents. They come from various authors, although they bear sufficient features in common to be grouped under the title of " Johannine literature."

The Fourth Gospel is different from the Synoptics in many

respects. First, it uses a plan of its own: instead of relating in order the Galilean ministry of Jesus, his itinerant activity in the northern territories, and his brief appearances in Judea before his arrest and death, the whole covering hardly more than seven or eight months in A.D. 29–30, the Fourth Gospel represents Jesus traveling several times between Jerusalem and Galilee in the course of three years. Secondly, it omits most of the miracles, recording only seven of them, which are peculiarly its own (especially the raising of Lazarus); it ignores the parables and the teaching on the Kingdom of God, the scenes in which Jesus is associated with despised classes, women, and children (the story of the adulteress [chs. 7:53 to 8:11] is not found in the early manuscripts), and even the important narratives on the baptism, the temptation, the Last Supper, and Gethsemane. Thirdly, it introduces long discourses, not found in the Synoptics, in which Jesus proclaims his pre-existence, his sinlessness, and his fearlessness; his passion and death appear in an unfolding drama of glorification. Thus the Gospel of John presents itself as an interpretation of the Christ, parallel to those which are found in the letters of Paul or in The Letter to the Hebrews. Christ is the Word of the Presence made flesh (ch. 1:4), which confers eternal life here and now (chs. 3:16; 4:14; 6:35; 10:10; 11:25; 12:25; etc.). The Last Day is still to come, but eschatological hope has been strained to such an extent that, "for the time being," unity with Christ transforms existence into a vitality that overcomes mortality.

In the words of Clement of Alexandria (third century), "After the other Evangelists had written the facts of history, John wrote a spiritual gospel." Who was the author? He may have been the "beloved disciple" (John 21:20) who often appears in the book, although never by name (chs. 13:23; 18:15; 19:26-27; 20:2-8; 21:7, 20), whom Irenaeus identified, in the second century, with John, the son of Zebedee, who would then have written in Ephesus at a very advanced age. However, a Syriac calendar of saints and martyrs declares that John was killed in Jerusalem before its destruction in A.D. 70, and we know that his brother was executed in A.D. 42 (Acts 12:2).

The evidence has been sifted for the past three centuries, and many scholars believe today that the work was done by a John the Elder, who lived at Ephesus at the end of the first century, and wrote also the three letters of John.

The Revelation to John is altogether different in style and content. Written by another John, exiled on Patmos, it is a Christian adaptation of Jewish apocalypses. Its aim is to comfort the bereaved. The letters (chs. 1 to 3) are addressed to seven churches of western Asia Minor. The world is coming to its end, and the Day of Light is at hand, with a new heaven and a new earth.

As in I Peter 5:13, Rome is described as the city of evil and the number 666 of the beast's name (Rev. 13:18) in all probability designates Nero or one of his successors, possibly Domitian. The book is a cry of faith in the Creator and an affirmation of life. Under its weird imagery, it proclaims the eschatological urgency of the Eucharist: " Come, Lord Jesus! "

The motif of the Presence that begat the literature of the Old Covenant also brought forth the literature of the New Covenant. But John saw no temple in the new Jerusalem, for " the tabernacle of God is with men " (Rev. 21:3).

We have followed the emergence of the entire Bible over more than a thousand years. Abraham's vision of a united humanity was yet a distant dream. The faith of Christianity was still oriented toward the New Age, where it contemplated the tree of life, whose leaves were for the healing of the nations.

From its beginning to its end, the literature of the Bible is the written Word by which the Presence ever creates a People.

CHAPTER 3 | *Canon, Text, and Versions*

Mᴀɴʏ of us take the English Bible for granted. We give hardly a thought to the eighteen hundred years or more that separate us from the latest writers of the New Testament. However, if we really accept the cardinal obligation of our faith, to love God with all our mind as well as with all our heart and will, we soon ask questions like these: Why are *these* sixty-six books in the Bible rather than other books? Who selected them? What was the principle of their selection? How were they transmitted to us? Who were "the keepers of the Word"? Can we be sure that the English words we read represent the thought of the original writers?

Such questions raise the problems of *canon, text,* and *versions.* No intellectually responsible Christian in our age can afford to ignore them.

I

The Greek term *kanōn,* "canon," was taken over from a Semitic word meaning "a reed stalk." It designated at first a measuring rod used by carpenters and builders, and it came to signify a standard of living and thinking. Paul himself used it in the sense of a rule of faith and behavior (Gal. 6:16; II Cor. 10:13-16). Christian writers of the third century, like Origen of Alexandria, applied it to *ta hagia biblia,* " the holy books." They meant of course the Hebrew Bible and the New Testament. They thought that such books had " authority," or were " canonical."

The ancient Hebrews preserved tables of stone on which " the Ten Words " (i.e., the Ten Commandments or Decalogue in the original short form) had been engraved (Ex. 24:4; see chs. 24:12; 31:18; 32:19; 34:1 ff.). Their sons, in the Land of Canaan, knew of codes of covenant law, written probably on sheepskin, which were kept in sanctuaries (Deut. 31:9-13; Josh. 24:25-26). Samuel wrote in a book the constitution of the kingdom, " and laid it up before Yahweh " (i.e., in a shrine, possibly that of Shiloh; I Sam. 10:25).

In 621 B.C., under the reign of Josiah, the priest of the Jerusalem Temple, Hilkiah, " found the book of the law," which was subsequently read aloud to the king. Its contents moved him so profoundly that he undertook a sweeping reform throughout the land (II Kings 22:3 to 23:25). It will be observed that " the book " itself needed to be authenticated before its contents were to be taken seriously, and the prophetess Huldah was thereupon consulted. The living oracle of Yahweh had to give sanction to a written document; the prophetic Word validated the written word (ch. 22:12-20). The idea of a " Bible " was born.

As scholars have shown (see Chapter 2), the " book of the law " discovered in 621 B.C. probably formed the core of Deuteronomy (chs. 12 to 26), possibly with other elements, such as the Decalogue and the Shema (chs. 5 and 6), as well as the Blessings and Curses (chs. 27 and 28; see II Kings 22:11).

Two centuries later (397 B.C.), the scribe Ezra came to Jerusalem with " the law in his hand " (Ezra 7:14, 25). It was by then the completed Pentateuch, which he read in a solemn assembly " from morning to midday " (Neh. 8:3). A similar "law" was preserved by the Samaritans in their own dialect.

By the time of Jesus ben Sirach, who wrote in Hebrew the book known as Ecclesiasticus (180 B.C.), and especially of his grandson, who translated it into Greek (about 130 B.C.), the three collections of the Law, the Prophets, and "other Writings" were read as "Scripture" in services of the synagogue, but their constitution and arrangement remained fluid. They did not form a closed body, and the openness of the "Scripture" was confirmed by the first Greek version of the Hebrew Bible.

As the Jews of the Diaspora, especially after Alexander the Great, adopted Greek as their native tongue, they needed to translate into that language the holy books of their fathers. Thus, the Greek Bible was born. It is known as the Septuagint (in abbreviation, the LXX), in honor of seventy-two elders who, according to a legend in the Letter of Aristeas (about 110 B.C.), wrote it in seventy-two days, in about 250 B.C., for the royal library of Alexandria. Internal evidence shows that the LXX translation was made, perhaps orally at first, over several generations of Greek-speaking worship in the synagogue services. It included the Pentateuch, the Prophets (Former and Latter, see Chapter 2), The Psalms, the other Writings, and also other books which we know as the Apocrypha. Certain manuscripts of the LXX even included a number of the so-called Pseudepigrapha; for example, the Prayer of Manasses, III and IV Maccabees, and possibly Enoch, IV Ezra, the Testaments of the XII Patriarchs, and the Psalms of Solomon (see Chapter 2).

In other words, there were among the Greek-speaking Jews a number of "canonical" books, but no "canon" in the sense of an official catalogue of books, except for the Pentateuch, or Law, and possibly also for the Prophets.

II

In the first century B.C., many Jews were accustomed to speak of "the Law and the Prophets" when they had in mind the sacred books of "Scripture" (II Macc. 8:23; etc.), and this usage appears frequently in the New Testament (Matt. 7:12; etc.). However, The Psalms are also quoted as authoritative (Matt. 21:42; etc.), and even once on a par with the Law and the Prophets (Luke 24:44). There are also in the New Testament several reminiscences and quotations of the books of the Greek Bible called Apocrypha, such as I Maccabees, Ecclesiasticus, the Wisdom of Solomon, and even from the Pseudepigrapha, like Enoch, the Assumption of Moses, and IV Ezra. Nevertheless, and this point is significant, although ignored by many modern historians of the Old Testament canon, these reminiscences and quotations of the Apocrypha and Pseudepigrapha are never presented as authoritative Scripture (i.e., with such a formula as "It is written").

In other words, in the time of the primitive church, there was no closed canon of the Old Testament for many Greek-speaking Jews of the Diaspora. At the same time, the early Christians, while using the Greek Bible, appear to have recognized as authoritative only those books which were subsequently a part of the Hebrew Bible in the Hebrew-speaking synagogues. Indeed, New Testament usage was confirmed by that which prevailed in about A.D. 95 at the Jewish college of Jabneh (Jamnia). It included all the books that are now in the Hebrew Bible, but none of the Apocrypha.

The early church fathers differed widely among themselves. Comparison of the lists of Melito of Sardis (about A.D. 170), Origen of Alexandria (about 250), Athanasius of Alexandria (329–339), and Jerome of Bethlehem (about 380), with the "canons" of the Syriac-speaking, Greek, Armenian, Coptic,

Abyssinian, and Latin churches reveals broad fluctuations of usage. The Latin church commonly read the Apocrypha alongside the other books of the Greek Bible, although Jerome, translator of the Vulgate, did not recognize the Apocryphal books in his list. The African synods (393, 397, and 419) admitted them under the influence of Augustine, but many scholars continued to express opposition to them.

Luther found them " good to read " but not authoritative, and they were included in Protestant Bibles until the beginning of the nineteenth century. The Roman Catholic Church did not include them officially in the canon of the Old Testament until the Council of Trent (1546). Many Roman Catholic scholars called them unofficially " deuterocanonical," i.e., of secondary importance. There has been a renewal of popular interest in the Apocrypha because of their significance for the understanding of Judaism before the time of Jesus.

III

The study of the canon of the New Testament presents comparatively simple problems, although elements of obscurity and complexity are not lacking. The history of the Hebrew Bible shows why the books of the early Christians could be added to the Jewish Scripture through a gradual process and without any awareness of creating a " brand new " collection. The first Christians grew up as Jews. They were accustomed to the authority of sacred books. They took for granted the idea of an authoritative Scripture. At the same time, they were not conscious of the completeness of a closed canon. The chronological overlapping in the formation of both Testaments offers the key to the understanding of the Christian Bible: it is a homogeneous expansion of the still-open Hebrew Scripture, which the primitive church interpreted by addenda. These additions, which eventually constituted the New Testament, were written through the living authority of the Christ, i.e., that of the words of Jesus (see I Cor. 7:10; 9:14) side by side with the "Word" of the Holy Spirit, the Comforter (John 14:26; see I Cor. 7:25-40).

At first the Christians had no intention of supplementing the Hebrew Bible, which they knew through the LXX, by new writings of their own. Indeed, the letters of Paul were simply notes addressed to specific communities. Nevertheless, they were soon copied and circulated for the edification of the churches. They became sources of inspiration in times of trial. They offered examples for the solution of new problems. They contained " standard " descriptions of the faith. Together with the Gospels, they were read during the celebration of the Eucharist, when the Word of the living Presence was again heard by the church at worship.

Until the middle of the second century A.D., however, the Gospels and epistles were authoritative on account of their contents, not because they were " Holy Scripture." The apostolic fathers knew them, but quoted them very freely (Clement of Rome, about 95; the Didache, 100; Ignatius, 110; Polycarp, 115; Barnabas, 120). In the early second century, according to Eusebius, Papias preferred the " living Word " to any book. A marked transformation appeared with Justin Martyr (163–167) and the principle of apostolic authorship. Certain writings, deemed to have been written by witnesses and apostles of the first generation, stood out from the others, and this principle was applied to the four Gospels and the letters of Paul.

Three factors played a part in this transformation: first, the Montanist movement in Asia Minor, with the excesses of its ecstatic prophets, made the church aware of the importance of the early tradition as a rule of faith and morals; second, the anti-Jewish Marcion rejected the Hebrew Bible entirely and made the church aware of a strictly Christian Scripture

(Marcion wanted one Gospel, similar to that of Luke, and the main epistles of Paul); third, many Gnostic sects, which combined the Christian message with a Hellenistic mystical philosophy, wrote books like the Gospel of Thomas, Valentinus' Gospel of Truth, and the Acts of John.

Reaction to this threefold menace led to the recognition of the four Gospels (Irenaeus, about 190), the main epistles of Paul, and later I Peter and I John. Melito of Sardis (about 170) had spoken of " the books of the Old Covenant," implying that the idea of " books of the New Covenant " was gaining access to the Christian mind.

Diversity of usage remained visible for a long time concerning the other books. For example, the Muratorian fragment (about 210) ignored Hebrews; Tertullian (about 230) attributed it to Barnabas, whereas Origen and Clement of Alexandria were inclined to see in it the work of a disciple of Paul. Gradually, Hebrews and the other General Epistles, together with The Revelation, were considered to be of apostolic origin. The present list of twenty-seven books first appears in the Easter letter of Athanasius (367).

The letters of Clement of Rome, Ignatius, and Barnabas, together with the Didache and the Shepherd of Hermas, which had enjoyed at some time or other " canonical " authority, were rejected. Fragments of other books form the Apocrypha of the New Testament.

It is significant to observe that the canon of the New Testament, like that of the Old, does not represent the formal action of an institution. Rather, the church was led gradually and progressively to enunciate a usage that imposed itself from within. The Christian will therefore discern in the canon the mysterious process by which the Holy Spirit witnesses to the Word.

IV

Like the study of the canon, the study of the text differs markedly for both Testaments. The manuscripts of the Hebrew Bible were minutely reproduced by the scribes (*sopherim*) of the first half of the first millennium A.D., and by their successors, the Masoretes (keepers of the Masorah, tradition) of the fifth to the ninth centuries A.D.

The Hebrew "alphabet," in which the manuscripts of the Old Testament were written, contained originally 22 letters, all consonants, and not a single vowel. The idea of a vowel sign is probably a Greek invention. This deficiency of the Hebrew "alphabet" presented grave problems of reading and interpretation. For example, the same three Hebrew letters, *D–B–R*, could be read *DaBaR*, "word," *DiBBeR*, "he spoke," *DeBeR*, "plague," *DoBeR*, "pasture," etc. In addition, the manuscripts crowded all the consonants together without space between words and without punctuation between clauses and sentences. To be sure, an oral tradition of correct pronunciation was carefully maintained, but the need for vowel signs, musical notation, and accents of punctuation became imperative. The Masoretes introduced into the "Consonantal Text" (still used exclusively in synagogues) ten vowel signs and many musical and punctuating accents. The result of their work has been called the "Masoretic Text."

Whereas the *sopherim* had corrected the Consonantal Text in eighteen passages (to prevent offensive sounds or ideas in public chanting), the Masoretes respected it scrupulously, but freely introduced thousands of corrections in the margins of the manuscripts. Most of these corrections involve only spelling, but a number of them affect meaning. For example, according to the Consonantal Text, Job cries out in a moment of defiance, "Behold, [God] may kill me, I shall not tremble [or 'hope']!"

(Job 13:15.) By changing one letter in the margin, the Masoretes permit the pious reading, " I shall hope in him," and the King James Version offers on this basis the sublime but premature exclamation of faith at all cost: " Though he slay me, yet will I trust in him." The original text is far more powerful, for it shows a man in defiance and yet in faith.

V

Sometimes the Masoretes did not find it necessary to indicate corrections in the margin. With words commonly used, they simply put with the consonants of the text the vowels of a different word that they proposed as an oral substitute. The most famous and unfortunate example occurs with the divine name " Yahweh." The Masoretes wrote the consonants YHWH with the vowels of the word " Adonai," " Lord," the spoken euphemism of the unutterable tetragrammaton. Thus arose in the Middle Ages the mistaken reading " Jehovah " (consonants of one word with the vowels of another).

The discovery of the Dead Sea scrolls (a consonantal text of some books, such as Isaiah, and fragments of many others), since 1947, has confirmed in part the accuracy of the Masoretic Text, although a number of Qumrân manuscripts reveal important variants (for example, I Sam., ch. 1, appears at Qumrân to follow a Hebrew text similar to that reflected by the LXX, which differs from the Masoretic Text at this point).

The science of textual criticism requires laborious efforts and immense learning. No translation or interpretation of the Old Testament can be carried out without a scientifically recovered text. In this difficult task, textual critics gather all the available witnesses and seek to reconstruct the original text out of all the variants according to well-defined " laws " of probability. This means in effect that they must compare the Hebrew manuscripts with one another as well as with the ancient versions

— the Samaritan Pentateuch; the Aramaic Targums (oral translations made in the Aramaic-speaking synagogues); and the Greek, Syriac, Latin, Coptic, Armenian, and Ethiopic versions.

VI

The Greek manuscripts of the New Testament present different problems. About 4,500 of them are known, and it has been estimated that they contain together about 150,000 variant readings, more than the number of New Testament words!

The earliest known manuscripts are fragmentary. They include a fragment with John 18:31-38, written in Egypt before A.D. 150. (Rylands Papyrus 457), a collection of the letters of Paul, also made in Egypt in the early part of the third century A.D. (Beatty-Michigan Papyrus in Dublin and Ann Arbor), and various excerpts from the Gospels, The Acts, and The Revelation. The earliest surviving copy of the complete New Testament dates from the fourth century (Codex Sinaiticus, in the British Museum, discovered in 1853 and 1859 at the St. Catherine Monastery in Sinai by Tischendorf). Another is almost complete (minus Heb. 9:14 to 13:25, the Pastorals and The Revelation [Codex Vaticanus, in the Vatican Library]). There are also an almost contemporary copy of the four Gospels (Freer Codex, in Washington), a fifth-century copy of the Gospels and Acts (Codex Bezae, in Cambridge), a fifth-century copy of the Bible (Codex Alexandrinus, in the British Museum), and a sixth-century copy of the letters of Paul (Codex Claromontanus, in the Bibliothèque Nationale in Paris). While the great manuscripts of the early period, like the Sinaiticus and the Vaticanus were written in Greek capital letters (uncials), the thousands of later manuscripts used small cursive letters (minuscules). The former are generally far more accurate than the latter.

The ancient versions of the New Testament, like those of

the Old Testament, offer valuable early witnesses of the text, especially the Old Syriac Gospels (fifth century) and the Syriac Peshitta Codex (A.D. 464, both in the British Museum). Jerome's translation of the New Testament into Latin (A.D. 382) became in the West the main instrument of New Testament transmission, and the Greek text passed into almost complete oblivion during much of the Middle Ages. It was published by Erasmus in 1516 and in the *Complutensian Polyglot* of Cardinal Ximenes in 1517. The discovery of the Codex Alexandrinus in 1627, and of the Codex Sinaiticus in 1859, together with the sudden availability of the Codex Vaticanus a few years later, stimulated the establishment of a critical edition of the text. This work enlisted the attention of many scholars, notably F. Westcott, F. J. A. Hort, and Eberhard Nestle, whose *Novum Testamentum Graece* (1912), periodically revised, has become a useful tool of study in the twentieth century. A new project, known as the " International Greek Testament," was begun in 1948 and is being carried out on the widest basis of manuscript investigation.

VII

It will be seen by this rapid survey that the " transmitters of the Word " form a mighty cohort whose work is not yet ended. Once again, the student of the Bible faces an element of historical relativity that intervenes not only in the composition, selection, and transmission of the books but also in their translation into modern languages.

Christian readers of the English Bible must remember that the King James Version, supreme as it remains in our time, was not dictated word for word from heaven. Translations are always betrayals. They are at best secondhand, dim, and cracked mirrors of the image they reflect. But they place the Word at the disposal of the People, and they are indispensable.

The earliest translation of the Bible in English was made from the Latin by John Wycliffe at the end of the fourteenth century. It was, however, the work of William Tyndale (1525–1536), of George Joye (1534–1535), and especially of Miles Coverdale (1537) that opened the Bible to the English-speaking world. Coverdale's Psalter remains to this day the translation used in the Book of Common Prayer.

The influence of Tyndale and of Coverdale maintained itself upon the subsequent editions of the English Bible: Taverner's Bible (1539), the Great Bible (1539), the Geneva or "Breeches" Bible (1560), the Bishops' Bible (1568), the Roman Catholic Douai-Reims Bible (1582–1610), and the King James Version (1611).

The King James Version, "the noblest monument of English prose" (John Livingston Lowes), is essentially a revision of the translations of Tyndale and of Coverdale, and met considerable opposition for many years.

Although its spelling has been thoroughly modernized, many of its words have become obsolete. Moreover, progress in textual criticism as well as in the knowledge of the Biblical languages (Hebrew, Aramaic, and *Koinē,* or "common," Greek) through the archaeological discovery of thousands of inscriptions and the development of comparative linguistics rendered a revision of the King James Version advisable. The English Revised Version appeared in 1881 and the American Standard Version in 1901.

Individual scholars made their own contributions, some of which stand out by their accuracy and brilliance: for example, the New Testament translation of R. F. Weymouth (1903), the translation of the Bible by James Moffatt (1913-1935), and the American Translation under the editorship of J. M. P. Smith and E. J. Goodspeed (1931).

The Revised Standard Version (1946–1952) represents a

reliable instrument of study. It aimed at converting the English of the King James Version into contemporary English while taking into account the latest discoveries in textual criticism.

The New English Bible (New Testament, 1961; Old Testament, in progress) represents the latest, but certainly not the last, attempt to turn the Bible into the English vernacular of the day. Unlike the American Revised Standard Version, it is an entirely " new " translation. It often compels the reader to sit up, to stop, and to listen, because its style, like our age, can be blunt. Yet, it strangely mixes literary stateliness (" truckling to no man," Matt. 22:16) with colloquialism (" I never sponged upon you," II Cor. 12:13), sometimes in the same context (" And with him went Mary who was betrothed to him. She was pregnant," Luke 2:6; see John 6:60!).

The Revised Standard Version and the New English Bible offer invaluable help in the understanding of hitherto obscure passages, especially in the letters of Paul, but it may be predicted that they will not survive much beyond the present generation.

Some scholars and churchmen agree with many lay lovers of the English tongue in calling for a restrained revision of the King James Version, which would emend erroneous and incomprehensible passages, but preserve those

> " Words that have drawn transcendent meanings up
> from the best passion of all by-gone time."

No version of the Bible will ever offer a meaning that is at once faithful to the original and self-evident to the reader.

CHAPTER 4 | *Manners of Interpretation*

CHRISTIANS read the Bible because they are brought thereby into the presence of the living God, confirmed as members of his people, and enabled to " hear " his word. Scripture has become for them the vehicle of the word of God. Nevertheless, it is first of all a literary and a historical monument.

I

The initial task of the reader of Scripture is to open his senses to the rigor and to the beauty of the literary forms. Anything that rings true creates its own style of expression, in horror, in exquisiteness, or in sublimity. Truth in literature cannot be reached without the reader's perception of words, phrases, lines, and strophic and rhetorical movements. It requires not only his comprehending faculties but also his aesthetic involvement — his artistic immersion within a literary mood, so that not only the written words but also the silences, the rhythms, and the climaxes may reach him across the centuries.

We shall delight in the art of the Hebrew storytellers, and we shall appreciate their ability to convey inner emotion with an utmost economy of devices. We shall soon perceive that the limpidity of their tongue and the soberness of their *métier* testify to the passion of their conviction.

65

Let us take one example that seems to stand on the periphery of our theological concern. Students of comparative literature maintain that romantic love as a literary motif arose only during the Middle Ages. Note, however, the instant of " recognition " when the eyes of a young man and a young woman meet for the first time (Gen. 24:63-64). We may follow the theme in the story of creation (Gen. 2:24); in The Book of Ruth; in The Song of Songs; in the theological imagery of the prophets, especially Hosea. The theologians of the Old Covenant could never have compared the loyalty — broken and yet maintained — of God and his people to the wonder of married love if the theme of romantic passion had not been deeply rooted in the consciousness of the nation. Indeed, the theology of mutual love, with its exclusive element, between Yahweh and Israel, presupposes a literature of total love between man and woman.

We shall also let our aesthetic faculties respond to the countless lines of poetry found in the pages of the Old Testament, from David's lament (II Sam. 1:21) to the cosmic questions addressed to Job from the whirlwind (Job 38:31), or even the satire of the prophet over the demise of the Babylonian potentate (Isa. 14:12). In each case, the analysis of the language reveals an articulation that is peculiarly suited to the intention of the poet.

Above all, it will be imperative for us to discover the poetic form — not only imagery and rhythm, but also strophic architecture — in order to isolate the literary units, seize the movements of thought, and discern the relative emphases. In such an archaic piece as Ps. 29, for example, which probably reaches beyond the time of David to the second millennium B.C., only the literary analysis will permit the interpreter to perceive the theme, which is arched between a prelude and a postlude anticipating the Christmas chorus of Luke: Gloria in Excelsis Deo and In Terra Pax.

The formal quality of the New Testament books is not generally on a similar level of literary excellence. They did not grow out of the epic age of a culture, when literature belonged to a folk aristocracy of windswept deserts. On the contrary, they were composed in a time of cultural decadence, and — as we have already seen — most of them represent circumstantial writing. Their authors were, by and large, unlettered laborers and tradesmen. Although Paul was a highly educated Jew, his concern in writing cannot be confused with a penchant for *belles-lettres!* Nevertheless, there are many literary gems in the New Testament also.

The parables of Jesus are vignettes of ellipsis, sometimes edged with whimsical irony. For example, to the Pharisees and scribes who murmured when he shared meals with prostitutes, collaborationists, and other so-called "sinners" (we would say "Communists and fellow travelers"), he told a parable in the form of a question: "What man of you, having a hundred sheep, if he has lost one of them, does not leave the ninety-nine *in the wilderness* . . . ? " (Luke 15:3). Only the most exact analysis of the parable *in its context* will reveal its point. The Aramaic or Hebrew rhetoric of Jesus still appears in the Sermon on the Mount, where investigation of the phraseology and sentence structure shows processes of development by repetition of thesis and antithesis (for example, Matt. 5:43-48). Jesus had mastered the skill of teaching by questioning, the science of epigrammatic summing up, and the art of invective attack that provoked response rather than resentment. He was not a writer, but his mastery over words surpasses at times that of the Old Testament storytellers and poets. Obviously, this kind of poetic prose deserves, on the part of the reader, an extremely careful study before its interpretation and especially its application may be ventured. The same remark applies to the discourses of The Acts, the lengthy discussions of

Paul, and the architectonic monument of the Fourth Gospel, in which one part balances another as in a Ravenna mosaic. The Lucan gospel of the Nativity cannot be approached like the Lucan account of the trial and execution: in each case, literary form dictates a peculiar manner of interpretation. Again, the impassioned pleas of Paul for freedom (from ritual obligations and moral pride, which he calls " garbage," Phil. 3:8), require on the part of the reader a frame of mind that is different from that which is required by Paul's triumphant affirmations of faith (I Cor. 15:53).

Manners of interpretation always partake of literary aesthetics. The reader will be careful to remain alert to every nuance of the verbs, sensitive to every accent of the writer's verve, and ever aware of the miracle of literary articulation: the indissolubility of the embrace between thought and form. Literature creates artistic empathy before it discloses its meaning. Literary analysis and appreciation constitute the first prerequisite of Biblical interpretation.

II

At the same time, the Christian reader will remember that Biblical aestheticism cannot be an end in itself, for the Bible is not concerned with " art for art's sake." It borrows elegance only to clothe truth, but it does not refrain from exposing a truth unadorned or ugly. The Bible is not only literature; it is also history, raw and sometimes even lewd.

The will to see the ancient Hebrews or the early Christians alive on the planet Earth constitutes the second prerequisite of Bible interpretation. We must involve ourselves in the historical concreteness of the people of God, which began in Ur of the Chaldees and continued — but did not end — on an executioners' hilltop.

We must therefore take full advantage of the discoveries

of archaeologists, linguists, literary and historical critics, geographers, and historians. The knowledge of the Code of Hammurabi, for example, and that of a score of other legal documents of the ancient Near East have radically altered our approach to the study of law and covenant. Unearthed inscriptions of the ninth and eighth centuries B.C. tell us of the time when "the Assyrian came down like a wolf on the fold." Israel and the church were brought forth in a world of conflict that is our world. We cannot begin to read the Bible unless we are willing to know the political, sociological, economic, religious, and other cultural factors that molded peoples and events in the ancient Near East and the Roman Empire.

For many students, the discovery of the Bible as history amounts to a kind of intellectual and spiritual "revelation." Someone told a lecturer, recently, with unabashed naïveté and the glow of existential excitement: "I had never suspected until today that the Bible was speaking of real persons." While history never repeats itself, essential similarities endure: pride in individuals, classes, races, nations; the quest for power and the psychology of self-deceit; the immorality of being certain to remain morally right; the pathetic search for self-identity and security or the ability of religion to make gods; and then, over against the ludicrously boring aspects of selfishness, the claims of the spirit, the heroism of humaneness, the purity of gratitude, the responsibilities of freedom, the miracle of self-giving love.

The Bible knows dishonesty in market speculation, shortcuts in the administration of justice, crimes for political reasons, or, even worse, for theological ones! It shows children playing and dying in the streets. It is aware of conflicts in loyalties and of the complexity of ethical decisions. It discerns degrees in good and in evil. It even grasps the ambiguities of either good or evil. Yahweh calls a monster like Nebuchadnez-

zar " my servant " (Jer. 43:10). He hails a somewhat enlightened barbarian like Cyrus the Persian as " [his] messiah " (Isa.
45:1). The world of the Bible is the world of history.

Depth psychologists are even looking at the books of the Old
and of the New Testaments as a source for the study of the
archetypal unconscious mind of man. While such a study is
still in its infancy, there is little doubt that it will yield in time
valuable clues for our understanding of the human psyche.

Our ancestors believed until the nineteenth century that the
Bible was a unique book in the literature of mankind. Many
of our contemporaries have given up this belief, but they
should beware of the fragility of their position, for a new development is taking place in our age. Thanks to the most
rigorous application of the historical method, even non-Christian historians have come to discern some unique characteristics among the Hebrews in the midst of the nations of the
classical Orient, and to discern the specific element of Christian faith in the religious chaos of the Roman Empire.

We shall therefore read the Bible as a historical document.
But if we read it only as literature for its art, or only as history for the information it offers us on the genesis of our
spiritual heritage, we are likely to misunderstand altogether
its own concept of history.

An exclusively historical approach to Scripture tends to produce paradoxically two opposite and mutually exclusive results.
On the one hand, it places us in the position of witnesses, ob-
serving a resurrected past with a hitherto unsuspected realism. On the other hand, it tends precisely to confine the Bible
to that remote past, thereby removing us from the Presence
that created it, isolating us from the People who wrote it, and
silencing in effect the Word that brought it forth. To look at
the Bible historically is in some ways to separate oneself from
its Word. It is to occupy the position of an outsider. A Christian

approach to Scripture does not neglect the literary and historical manners of interpretation, but it proceeds beyond them. Historicism, like aestheticism, is the trap that awaits many readers of the Bible. There is still another.

III

At this time, we have to consider a manner of interpretation that pays lip service and even heart service to the idea of the Bible as the word of God but that violates the dynamic quality of Biblical faith itself. It is the trap of Biblicism.

A basic fallacy lies at the root of what is popularly and mistakenly known as a Protestant " principle " par excellence: namely, that the individual believer needs only to be alone with the Holy Scriptures to find light. No responsible theologian has ever formulated or endorsed this idea. Luther was aware of the abuses of subjectivism in Biblical interpretation. He said: " Today, everybody claims to be a ' Master in Scriptures ' . . . while in all other trades and arts one has monitors."

The Pharisees who attacked Jesus for healing a man on the Sabbath were sincere in their respect for the Hebrew Bible, but their obedience to the law apparently conferred upon them a sense of satisfaction that set them apart from the needs of the common people. Their Biblicism concealed their desperate quest for security and rendered them insensitive to the total demand of God. Their fidelity to the Bible had become a form of idolatry, for they transformed the insecurity of faith into the false security of moral and ritual purity. The Pharisaic attitude has remained throughout the centuries the sin above all of Christians, be they Catholic or Protestant.

The Bible was carefully preserved in the medieval and Renaissance church, but the Biblical call for faith as the total response of man to a grace that can never be forced, earned, or deserved appears to have been often ignored. For many, the observance of piety had become a way of securing riches in this world and happiness in the world to come. In the sixteenth century, the church as always hailed the Holy Bible. It officially proclaimed that Scripture offered the revelation of God to mankind, as much as the Jews did in New Testament times, but the dynamic character of a human hope ever pinned on the mercy of a present God did not readily appear in the ecclesiastical sales of indulgences. Nor did the theologians of the Inquisition reveal a " Christian " manner of Biblical interpretation when they justified the violence of their methods by the word of Jesus in the parable of the great banquet: " Compel [them] to come in! " (Luke 14:23).

Luther, the Augustinian monk, like Paul, the Pharisee, had been shattered and transformed into a new man by the experience of a faith that earned nothing and demanded all (Rom. 5:1).

The Protestant Reformation was chiefly due to the rediscovery through Scripture of the gratuitous love of God. Men again read the Bible and " heard " a very present God speak to the needs of their guilt, the anguish of their despair, or the folly of their respectability.

There have been and there are still, in the life of Judaism and of the universal church, places and times when men read the Bible as if blindfolded (II Cor. 3:14). There are other places and times when the veil is lifted. The same words become the channel of a direct, immediate confrontation between a God who offers himself and a man who responds with the whole of his existence.

The thrill of our age — Christians will say, the only source of its hope — is to participate in the present renewal of Biblical dynamism. Such a renewal can be witnessed among Jews, chiefly through the work of Martin Buber and his followers, and also among Roman Catholics. Begun at the end of the nineteenth century mainly by Dominicans, the Scriptural revival in the Roman Catholic Church is now worldwide.

Among Protestants, ecclesiastical Biblicism has often led to strange perversions of Christian thought. Any view on almost any subject may be " based " on some isolated passage of the Bible (while the rest of it is carefully ignored). For example, some have justified Scripturally such antithetical views as capitalism and communism, militarism and pacificism, internationalism and nationalism, monarchy and democracy, ecclesiastical authoritarianism and nonconformism, sacramentalism and nonsacramentalism, and polygamy and monogamy as well as virginity.

A confusion may be seen in the popular Protestant mind (Jewish and Roman Catholic too) between interpretation and application. Biblicism is the aberration, either of a group or of an individual, that takes the Bible as an end in itself, makes of it an absolute, and confuses it with God himself. Bibliolatry is just another form of idolatry — one of the manifold manifestations of man's uncanny ability to manufacture gods, especially in times of cultural decay and fear.

The Bible does not provide us with a blueprint for living, but it changes us by ushering our destitute selves into the presence of a holy God. A literary and historical approach to Scripture will inevitably lead the Christian reader to face the theological manner of interpretation.

IV

The study of Scripture is in the end a theological activity that involves the spirit and the will as much as the emotions and the intellect. " Theo-logy " is not a science in some special fragment of the natural world. It is the " knowledge " of God in the sense of a personal communion between the infinite Reality and a finite individual. Something happens to this finite individual if the bond of communion with the infinite Reality is genuine. The Christian interpreter of Scripture is willing to take risks when he reads its pages, precisely because he reads Scripture as part of his act of communion with the infinite Reality.

The Christian interpreter of Scripture therefore will not stifle his artistic and intellectual faculties. On the contrary, he will use their power of knowing to the full, but he will emerge from a mere concern for enjoyment or learning. He will give up the sense of his intellectual security. He will be ready to move from any cherished *status quo*. In the presence of the Creator of the universe, he will learn personally from the Bible his own predicament and his eternal destination.

A theological manner of interpretation depends upon our becoming new creatures and members of the ongoing people of God in history. We shall be careful not to repeat too easily that the Bible is the inspired word or the revelation of God to man, because we know that such a declaration, if it is to be other than passive acceptance of traditional language, must originate from the brokenness and rebirth of our very selves.

The Christian interpreter of the Bible in a concrete sense is a participating actor in the drama of history. A theological interpretation means the enlistment of the interpreter. Theology is knowledge of God by a man who worships God in the time-and-space-transcending church. I cannot know God unless I adore him, and I adore him surrounded by the witnesses who precede, accompany, and follow me. A theological interpretation is inseparable from the act of adoration, when historical time becomes the time of God.

Only on the surface is time a duration of chronology. In the act of adoration, before the face of the Holy God and in the midst of the People that counts within its ranks all generations of men from Abraham to the end of history, the Christian reader of the Bible transcends chronological sequence and participates in the time of God.

From the standpoint of chronological or clock-and-calendar time, the history of the Hebrews and of the early church belongs to a dead past, together with the gory splendors of Nineveh and Thebes. From the vantage vision of liturgical time, however, Scripture becomes the vessel that contains the living drama of our salvation.

In the prologue of this drama, Abraham, the Hebrew, becomes the father of the faith, because he left the safety of his ancestors' home and faced, in obedience to his vision of ultimate permanence, the risks of the totality of his existence.

In the first act, the Hebrews abandon the fleshpots of Egypt for a forty years' Lent in the wilderness, to engage there in a bond of loyalty and gratitude to a Presence that delivers them not only from the slavery of tyrants but also from the tyranny of their own beings.

In the second act, the sons of the Hebrews " fill their bellies " in the land of plenty and at the same time break there the covenant of fidelity to a holy mode of living: their historical rise and fall become the revelation of the grace and the judgment that always preside over the affairs of men.

In the third act, Judaism is born in the agonies of national death, but its new hopes are frozen into racial, legal, and ritual particularism: the Servant of the Lord in history repudiates his mission to the nations of the world.

In the fourth act, a son of Judaism, a member of the human race who is " born of a woman," rises up to the summons to be servant and is by men rejected. He " suffered under Pontius Pilate, was crucified, dead, and buried; he descended into hell." The drama reaches its supreme irony: the hopes of man are crushed by man.

The fifth act starts with Easter. when the disciples of the

man Jesus rally not to his dead memory but to his living Presence, and recognize in him the Word made flesh, Christ the Lord, the living Head of the living body of which, to their utter bewilderment, they form an organic and ongoing part.

The above comparison of the acts of God to a drama is inadequate, but it may help to point to the theological interpretation of Scripture, which is itself an interpretation of history by faith. The Christian interpreter knows that, in this drama, the fifth act is now playing! It has, in fact, just begun. And he, the interpreter, is part of it.

The epilogue is at the end of history, when God will be " all in all." Liturgically, the epilogue has already been enacted, although outside of the act of worship it is still to come. The life of the church is eschatological. It extends between Easter and the end of history. Chronological time is not erased. History remains the theater of man's existence. Nevertheless, at the moment of worship, the past and the future are brought together in the present reality of God. While the psalmists could, in the act of adoration within the esplanades of the Jerusalem Temple, contemplate the Kingdom of God as a *fait accompli,* they knew very well that violence and war, at that very instant, were tearing men apart and threatening their own existence. Yet they sang: " The princes of the nations are gathered together as the people of the God of Abraham " (Ps. 47:9).

It is not by coincidence that the early church, thrown into the historical realism of the Roman Empire, which is still the arena of our own existence, sang the same hymn in the celebration of the ascension of the risen Christ. Liturgically, they lived — and so do we — in the time of God. In the act of worship, history has come to its fulfillment. " Behold, now is the accepted time; behold, now is the day of salvation! " (II Cor. 6:2.)

The " Day of Yahweh " expected by the prophets, that is to

say, the day of judgment, has become the new Sabbath, the day of new creation, " the Lord's Day."

V

Because he is at once the observer of Scripture and a participant in the drama of Scripture, the theological interpreter will take cognizance of the peculiar nature of his responsibilities.

In the first place, he will be profoundly aware of the mystery of divine Presence that pervades the Bible. He will enter its world with awe and open expectation. But such an attitude shall never be confused with intellectual obscurantism. Reverence and humility will prevent the reader of the Bible from interpreting with the illusion of omniscience, but they must never be divorced from intellectual integrity.

One of the reasons for which Christian faith is rejected *in depth* by the majority of our contemporaries, even by those who belong to some church or declare in the so-called polls of public opinion that they believe in God, must be ascribed to the lack of intellectual integrity that the Christian church, along with Judaism, often shows in interpreting Scripture.

In the second place, the theological interpreter will recognize the unity of the Bible as a dynamic and organic unity. On the one hand, the church of the first hour knew that Jesus brought in his person a new gospel and a new law: " You have heard that it was said to the men of old, . . . but I say to you . . ." (Matt. 5:21-22, etc.) On the other hand, the same Evangelist preserved with these sayings the preface: " Think not that I have come to abolish the law and the prophets; I have come not to abolish them but to fulfil them " (Matt 5:17). Here is symbolically expressed the double principle of continuity and discontinuity.

The literary and historical diversity of Scripture will therefore be taken with utmost seriousness. " In many *and various*

ways God spoke of old to our fathers by the prophets." (Heb.
1:1.) Chronological time is not erased. Circumcision, sacrificial
offerings, laws of impurity, curses in The Psalms, "divine"
commands to steal jewels from the Egyptians (Ex. 11:1-2) or
to exterminate "both man and woman, infant and suckling"
of the Amalekites (I Sam. 15:3) will be viewed in the perspective of the agonies of a God who strove to make himself
known *in time* to the family of man. Therefore, anecdotes on
the patriarchs, the judges, and the kings, which reflect strange
levels of belief or morals, will not be explained away by the
use of the allegorical, spiritual, or mystical "interpretation."
Such a method represents a denial of the divine mode of self-
disclosure, which respects history. It lacks, furthermore, any
objective basis of operation.

In the third place, the theological interpreter of Scripture
will discern that the principle of continuity between the two
Covenants arises from a study of the Hebrew Bible itself. A
mood of intense expectation pervades all its parts — Law,
Prophets, and Hagiographa. A passionate hope for God's full
entrance into human existence inspires all the poets, writers,
and editors of the Old Testament. Creation calls for its perfec-
tion. The end becomes a new beginning: in technical language,
the Old Testament is at once protological and eschatological.
In spite of the earthly Temple, with its sacramental experience
of liturgical time, the prayer of the covenant-breaking people
(Jer. 31:31) remains the same — for priests, prophets, and wise
men alike. "Show me, I beseech thee, thy glory," cries Moses
(Ex. 33:18); "Oh that thou wouldest rend the heavens, that
thou wouldest come down," exclaims the poet in Third Isaiah
(Isa. 64:1); and the Job who is Everyman echoes, "If only
there were a mediator betwixt us that might lay his hand upon
us both!" (Job 9:33).

A stringency of theological demand is at once the burden

and the glory of the people of God. Far more than a "messiah" of Davidic line who would rule with equity (Isa. 9:2-7; 11:1-9; etc.) or "one like a son of man" who would fight from above with the heavenly hosts (Dan. 7:13), the Old Testament asks for "the enormous Divine" that shares its transcendence over the cosmos with the incredible immanence of God's very self within the human heart (Isa. 57:15). In the words of the Jewish theologian Martin Buber: "The Absolute Power is for human personality's sake become personality. . . . He offers himself . . . as an answer."

By knowing God as real Being, compared to a husband who loves a woman in her unfaithfulness (Hos. 3:1 ff.; etc.), to a father who cannot forget his perverted sons (Isa. 1:2; etc.), to a mother whose compassions are kindled ever to forgive (Isa. 66:13; etc.), the Old Testament is possessed by the fever of waiting for the humanity of God. It wants a shepherd risking his life for his sheep (Ezek. 34:12; etc.).

The church was born when a Jew was recognized by Jews as the answer to this hope. This is the reason for which "we are spiritually Semites." Then Christianity exploded the confines of a Judaism folded upon itself, and sought the extremities of the earth.

Incarnation is the gift of Israel to Christianity. To recognize it as the central event of history is the key to the understanding of the unity of the Bible and its relevance. To live the incarnation in the church's historical existence is the mission of the church and the only source of her vitality.

Such a consideration leads the theological interpreter to look at the Bible as "a true and live myth," through which both the universe and the history of man — this means you and me — are brought within the compass of the act of God. The word "myth," however, requires definition.

CHAPTER 5 | *The Sacrament of the Word*

THE church is not merely a society of believers: it is the living body of Christ in history, and this body takes historical reality as well as the consciousness of itself in the celebration of the Eucharist. It remains alive, faithful, pure, and active only in the measure with which it is the incarnation of the Word. Its mission is to proclaim the Word by living it.

I

The vitality of the church depends upon the sacrament of the Word. A sacrament is the sensible sign of the gift of God to man. So also is the Bible, the readable manifestation of the Word that the Presence addresses to his People. The sacrament of the Word assumes a dual form: the celebration of the Eucharist and the reading of Scripture.

Without God's presence sacramentally offered in the Eucharist, the Bible contains only the word of an absent God. Without the Bible, the Eucharist offers a Word-less presence that soon risks degenerating into the well-known perversions of Christendom: pantheistic mysticism, sentimental quietism, merit ritualism, spiritual mercantilism, social-club activism.

The Bible and the church therefore stand together in a relation of delicate mutuality. Historians of the text and canon

may say that the church made the Scripture, but such a statement merely skims over the surface of the history of Judaism
and of early Christianity. In depth, the Bible grew with the
church, always slightly ahead of her according to chronological
time. The church did not really " canonize " her own canon.
She officially recognized that the Scripture was canonical because it already constituted for her a test, a standard, a norm,
and a critique. Both the church and the Bible are different and
complementary manifestations of the Word. The Bible remains
the record of the church's origin, the " yardstick " of her fidelity. It is the Bible that judges the church, not the contrary. In
the testimony of the Bible, the church finds the cloth of her
worship, the substance of her thought, and the nerve of her
action. In the reading of the Bible as in the celebration of the
Eucharist, the church celebrates the memory of her birth, she
responds to the experience of her communion, and she antici-
pates her end by living it today.

The above statements, of course, are possible only within the
reality of Biblical faith, which uses an idiom of its own, and
which the contemporary mind, by and large, is inclined to dis-
miss as a manifestation of obsolete, mythical thinking. Such a
dismissal, however, reflects intellectual haste and confusion.

We shall readily admit that the whole vitality of the church
is in some sense mythical, for it relates its past, its present, and
its future to the Biblical myth, but we shall see that the Biblical
myth is endowed with a specific quality that sets it apart from
all other myths, because it interprets the cosmos and the history
of man in the light of three moments of divine activity: creation, incarnation, and new creation.

II

It is dangerous to speak of the mythical aspects of Biblical
faith, for the popular misunderstanding of the word assumes

that a myth is "something that is untrue." However, the Greek *mythos* designated originally the proclamation of the sacred word, which was uttered in a sanctuary during the celebration of a festival. Later on, it came to mean a fable or a fanciful tale about gods and goddesses (for example, the *Theogony* of Hesiod), but only when Western culture ceased from believing in the Greco-Roman deities. In modern times, the use of the word "myth" was revived by philosophers, historians of comparative religions, and especially psychologists in order to designate a form of concrete discourse whose aim is to describe a truth for which there cannot be any adequate formulation according to the processes of rational thinking. To speak of myth is to recognize in the depth of the human psyche the finiteness of the intellect and the demonic power of the unconscious drives (be they of a biological or an archetypal origin). It is also to be aware of the hidden bond between emotional and volitional behavior. This means that there are many kinds of myths: cosmic and psychological, anthropological and ethnological, and — from another perspective, which seeks to differentiate them by their effects — there are static and dynamic myths, disruptive and cohesive myths, dead and live myths. All cultures have their myths, whether they are archaic or modern. There are, for example, the myths of nationalism and internationalism, racialism and interracialism, democracy and fascism, Pan-Germanism and national socialism, Federalism and Marxist Communism, American Adamism (with its revolt of the "New Man" against the Old World corruption and its various nineteenth-century Utopias), Pan-Africanism, etc. Even natural science, as soon as it seeks to overcome the fragmentation of specialized analysis and attempts to correlate its knowledge of "nature" with a worldwide outlook, must use mythological language. Any depiction of truth that cannot be measured or empirically observed partakes of the myth-making processes. The cosmological hypotheses of contemporary astrophysicists stand on the edge of mythical discourse.

The Bible uses mythical language from its beginning to its end. It speaks of creation, both of the universe and of man, of the expulsion of Adam and Eve from the Garden of Eden, of the affairs of the sons of God with the daughters of men, of the fire and thunder on Mt. Sinai, of Zion as the "navel of the earth," of the Messianic paradise, of the fall of Lucifer, of the Last Day, of the birth of Jesus from the womb of a virgin, of his struggle with Satan, of his descent into the underworld, of his resurrection and ascension into heaven, of his second coming in glory, of the new heaven and of the new earth, of the millennium, of the heavenly Jerusalem, of the *plērōma* or "fulfillment" of all things. To be sure, not all these themes represent the same kind of mythical thinking — as we shall see — but all of them belong to a peculiar form of discourse, and some of them even assume a literary pattern akin to those of the Near Eastern and Hellenistic myths.

No well-informed and honest intellect can afford to ignore such affinities. At the same time, the reader of the Bible will observe the unique way in which both the ancient Hebrews and the primitive Christians, sons of their mythical age as they were, expressed a universal truth that concerns you and me.

The pagan myths attempted to describe *status quo* in space. That which has been remains today and shall be forever. The Bible, on the contrary, is "a true and live myth," because it relates the sacred word to the most dynamic view of history, *our history,* a history that moves from creation to re-creation through incarnation. Space myth is overcome by time myth, and this is the reason for which Scripture judges and gives life to the church in all centuries.

III

On the last Sunday after Trinity, at the end of the liturgical year and before the beginning of Advent, the church uses as the Introit to the celebration of the Eucharist: " Behold, the tabernacle of God is with men, . . . and they shall be his people."

The Lord's Supper is first of all an act of liturgical remembrance, which does not mean merely a recollection of the past by an act of detached memory but involves participation in the *time* of God's activity. Thus, the church, like the Bible, rehearses creation as the first part of the sacrament of the Word.

To remember creation is to live creation and to take one's stand within it. (Ps. 95:6-8.)

Modern study has shown that the priests of Jerusalem probably composed Gen., ch. 1, as a liturgy for the celebration of the new year festival at the autumnal equinox. Like the hymn of Ps. 104, which was sung on the same day, the Creation story is not a text of scientific knowledge but the proclamation of the covenant faith. A holy people at worship, buffeted by the empires and threatened with extinction, sings: " The Lord Omnipotent reigneth! " Archaic myths have left their traces in the Bible, but they have been " broken " by the Hebrew theology of the covenant, because they did not radically distinguish between the Creator and the created world. There is no " creation " myth, strictly speaking, outside of the Bible. Pagan myths did not hail a truly creative God. They sought in their cosmogonies (stories of the origin of the world) to explain their rituals of security and fertility. They attempted to make *space* secure and livable. Their cosmogonies were in fact indistinguishable from their theogonies (stories of the origin of the gods) and both usually took the form of theomachies (stories of combats between deified forces of chaotic life and deified forces of order). The pagan myths did not succeed in conceiving the idea of a creator, because they failed to see that the world is not divine or that God is not to be confused with the world. Their theologies had to be polytheistic, because their gods and goddesses were only mythical representations of natural powers — the sun, moon, and stars; the ocean, the Nile; the germination of seed, and animal and human sexuality. In the Biblical myth, on the contrary, there is neither theogony nor full-fledged theomachy (although the prophets [Isa. 51:9], the psalmists [Ps. 74:13; 89:9], and the Joban poet [9:13] allude to victory over the sea serpent in their poetic descriptions of Yahweh's omnipotence), because there is not the slightest room for a speculation about the birth of God, nor is there any doubt as to the completeness of his created act.

In the pagan myths, life is divine and preexistent, but chaotic. In the Bible, God has life and eternity, and he creates. Chaos is either created, as in Second Isaiah (ch. 45:7), Job (ch. 38:16), The Psalms (ch. 104:26; 146:6), or Proverbs (ch. 8:24-28), or else it is used as an intermediary motif that respects the mysterious power of evil, as in Gen. 1:2. There, the theme of the striving of the Spirit of God over the face of the deep represents the survival of the pagan myth of preexistent chaos, but its presence has a specific function to fulfill: the priests knew that evil remains a reality that threatens the cosmos and man, yet never God! The motif is incorporated in second place, after Gen. 1:1. Genesis 1:2 compares the creative activity, not to an act of procreation, but to the love of a mother bird teaching her young to fly by themselves. In addition, the motif is subsumed to that of creation by the word *Fiat*, " Let it be! "

Modern science does not make our faith in God the creator today more difficult than archaic myths did our fathers' faith yesterday. It is not science, whether in its prescientific or contemporary forms, that leads man to affirm (or deny) creation.

It is faith in a God who creates now. Ancient Israel did not learn first about creation, but she first responded to her historical call. She felt grasped by a power of healing and liberation. She knew a God who carried her " on eagles' wings " over the centuries of historical crises, and when she hit bottom during the exile in Babylon, when the entire Near East was the prey of cultural decay, when she was ready to give in to despair, she spoke the word: " In the beginning, God! " She could speak this word because she knew her destiny, which is the end of man. " And God made man in his image."

There is a closer affinity between God and man than between man and nature. Yet, man receives the challenge and the opportunity to fill the earth and to subdue nature. And this means the conquest of floods, or famine, of disease, and of space. It was on the strength of the gospel of the exodus that Israel could look at the wonders of heaven and earth, including the mystery of biological existence, knowing that her God was in absolute control of the elements. She expressed that faith in the myth of creation. Creation, however, represents only a challenge and an opportunity for man to live as the vice-regent of the universe. It is on account of her awe-ful mission toward all the people of the earth that Israel learned about the Creator.

Like Israel, the church hails God as the maker of heaven and earth because it knows him to be its savior, who elects it to work on his behalf. And it can hear the morning stars sing together and the sons of God shout for joy (Job 38:7) because it prays in the shame of its defeats: " Have mercy upon us! "

Here is the wonder of the myth of creation: in the sacrament of the Word, the Bible and the church begin by affirming the goodness of this world, and the hallowing of time in this history. Genesis, ch. 1, moves toward the mystery of the Sabbath. The discovery of truth about the world is only an incentive for man to make the whole of life holy for the Creator of life.

In the macrocosm of the swiftly expanding universe, the Lord of that universe is also the Lord of myself. The Bible does not tell us when and how the world began, but it inserts us in the time of God, which is now.

To hail God as the Creator is to take cognizance of one's mission in life. When we genuinely attempt to participate in the myth of creation, we do not merely drift at the edge of a metagalaxy, but we begin to live in God's present moment to the full. The Bible is " a true and live myth " of creation.

IV

The remembrance of the Eucharist is centered on the myth of the Incarnation: " Having in remembrance his blessed passion and precious death, his mighty resurrection and glorious ascension; rendering unto thee most hearty thanks . . ." However, such a reality is appropriated by faith through the sacrament of the Word only when the same faith is incorporated within the reality of the Fall.

There is a radical difference between the two, for the story of Adam and Eve in the garden is a myth introduced into history, whereas the story of the birth, ministry, death, and glorification of Jesus represents history introduced into myth. The first depicts the situation of man's existence, which is estrangement from God. The second proclaims the entrance of God into history for the reconciliation of man's existence with God's life. The history of our salvation is played in two gardens, one of delights where Adam fell and with him the whole of mankind, the other of agonies, where Jesus stood, and with him the whole of a new humanity.

A pagan myth is something that has never happened but happens every day. " This never was but always is," said Sallustius of the myth of Attis, whose death was mourned in the rites of spring. The remark is apt if it refers to the myth of

Adam, but it must be reversed if it is to apply to the myth of
Christ, for " this was, and therefore always is." The historicity
of God's intervention in man's life is at the center of the
Bible.

The myth of Adam remains " unbroken " if the Old Testament is cut off from the New. Here lies perhaps one of the
reasons for which traditional Judaism and modernist Protestantism have much in common. Neither of them takes the
tragic condition of man's existence seriously. Therefore, the
religion of Jesus as a model to imitate can be " salvaged " from
the myth of his death and resurrection. For Biblical Christianity, on the contrary, as for the ancient Yahwist, Adam is *'ādhām,*
" the Man," Everyman. It is no accident that the priestly
editor of the Pentateuch placed Gen., chs. 2 and 3, after Gen.,
ch. 1. Man is created in God's image. He is sufficiently like
God to be dissatisfied with man-made gods. His capacity for
self-transcendence is the source of his tragedy. He denies his
creatureliness and the finitude of his existence because he
knows enough to wish to know all (the expression " knowledge of good and evil " in Hebrew suggests the science of the
absolute). The desire of man is to be " like God." The eating of
the fruit does not symbolize the use of sexuality, unless it be as
a mystical technique for gaining the illusion of immortality.
Popular opinion mistakenly identifies sin and sexual delight.
In fact, man is a sinner whenever he wishes to be divine. The
fulfillment of this wish produces, paradoxically, total estrangement from God, from self, and from others. Sin is not sex but
estrangement. Alienation from God, however, manifests itself
at once in man's sexual shame, which becomes the symbol of
his destitution. His love for woman is vitiated by his separa-
tion from God. Other motifs, such as that of the serpent, which
symbolized in the Canaanite cultus the demonic powers of the
earth, are now made subsidiary to the main theme.

The totality of man's existence is one of labor in the sweat of his brow, until death comes and dust returns to dust. Sin is the will to do without God by becoming oneself a god (cf. Isa., ch. 14, and Ezek., ch. 28). Man is not really expelled from the garden: it is he who expels God from his universe. And his existence on earth is indeed one of rewardless labor. Cain slays Abel, Noah gets drunk, and men go a-building a tower to scale the heights. Estrangement from God breeds hatred, folly, and unreality. In spite of traditional Judaism and modernist Protestantism, original sin is no dead myth. It depicts the solidarity of mankind in the universality of the death wish, which prompts the church to sing with John Donne:

"Wilt thou forgive that sin where I begun,
Which is my sin though it were done before?"

From the Yahwist's picture of God looking at the heart of men and finding that "every impulse of their volitional schemes was only evil every day" (Gen. 6:5), to the prophets who knew the indelibility of a leopard's spots (Jer. 13:23) and the psalmists who lamented that "there is none that does good, no, not one" (Ps. 14:3), the Bible nurtures no illusion. Natural man moves swiftly and irreversibly "to the last syllable of recorded time," but "time's immutability" is reversed by the first hint of divine self-offer in Abraham's call to reckless adventure. Here holy history begins. The prophets are waiting for the end of time. They herald "a new covenant."

And then, God comes. The liturgy of the Eucharist, like the Gospels, literally explodes with the sound of the trumpets at the consecration of the Host: Hosannah in excelsis! The whole history of the old covenant is now ushered in as a witness to the mystery of incarnation. The sacrament of the Word made flesh supersedes the Temple. With the old Hebraic motif of cultic presence as a nomadic sojourn, the universal church becomes the universal shrine. Holy history takes the place of holy geography.

Considering that the object proper to Christian faith is not simply the God who intervenes in history but more precisely the Christ who appears in the person of Jesus, and that, furthermore, this person is fully historical, we find it normal to try the so-called historical approach. We do our best to see Jesus, but difficulties begin here.

The Gospels do not present a human being in his historical development of maturation, but they show a type already achieved, with its elements lifted up and carried to an absolute level, outside the domain of relativity, and therefore beyond the realm of history.

In the Gospels, Jesus is not only humble, but Humility; not only courageous, but Courage; not only severe, but Severity; not only merciful, but Mercy. He does not appear as an individual among others. Even Mark, supposedly the least " theological " of the Evangelists, opens his work with the words: " The beginning of the gospel of Jesus Christ, the Son of God." For the Evangelists themselves, Jesus was a man, truly and fully a man, a being of flesh and bones, who suffered and died upon a cross; yet they wrote the story not as a testimony to a personality of the past, but as a witness to the ever-present Christ.

Indeed, the life and teaching of Jesus, if we ever arrive at the knowledge of them, condemn us rather than save us, frighten us more than attract us, bring us to despair rather than hope. For Jesus required absolute commitment: " Ye shall be perfect, as your heavenly Father is perfect " (Matt. 5:48). The Sermon on the Mount, with its ethics of totality, is a source of unending torment. It can lead only to the cross.

The language of the Bible may be a stumbling block for many. The formulation of the mystery of redemption may not satisfy our minds. We may rebel at the traditional terms: propitiation, atonement, satisfaction, substitution, and others. We may repudiate dogmatic speculations that are derived from the Semitic beliefs in the sacrificial value of blood and are furthermore complicated by the paradoxical statements of the Nicene Creed: " Begotten of his Father before all worlds; God of God; Light of Light; Very God of Very God; begotten, not made; being of one substance with the Father, by whom all things were made; who for us men, and for our salvation, came down from heaven; and was incarnate by the Holy Ghost of the Virgin Mary, and was made man." This is the language of myth, and one cannot translate it into rational formulation without losing the core of the Gospel, which glows in the naïve formula: " Jesus died for me."

Even non-Christian students of the origins of Christianity acknowledge the fact that it is not the gospel that preserved the mystery of the cross. On the contrary, it was the mystery of the cross that preserved the gospel. There is a remarkable diversity of religious experiences and of theological beliefs in the New Testament, but there is also a remarkable unity as far as the meaning of the death of Jesus is concerned. Not only Paul and John but all the early Christians preached Jesus crucified. We may try to shun the issue. We may succeed in ignoring it most of the year, even sometimes on Good Friday. It remains that early Christianity was first and last a religious mystery of the daily dying and rising of the self, in identification by faith with the dying and rising Lord, and modern Christianity cannot be otherwise.

A Servant: this is the God whom we are called to serve. His method is peculiar, indeed. His challenge to endurance is a description of himself. He chooses a people as a witness, not because they have a genius for religion or a knack for morality. He knows full well that Israel and the church are a stiff-necked people, and that their hearts are stones. He endures them to the end, and although they bring him sweet cane with money, they enslave him with their iniquities. That is the reason for which he comes to us under the form of a slave. And while he hangs there, attached to the wood, we still command: "Save yourself!" But he stays there.

We see in him the image of a God who takes upon himself the estrangement and the final insecurity of our existence. His life becomes the passion of God himself in the midst of our humanity. One cannot grasp the pathos of God apart from the incarnation. The story of Bethlehem belongs to Holy Week.

God has never abandoned his creature, even and precisely when he is silent. He is at work in this world. What is new and unique in Biblical faith is that "God is so much God that he can be more than eternal, namely, temporal; more than God, namely, man. While the divine word, to make itself heard of men, adopts human existence, it hides and conceals its divinity in opprobrium and [mockery]. In proposing itself to our faith, it exposes itself to scandal. It is the . . . wonder of our rebirth" (Karl Barth, *Die Lehre vom Worte Gottes*, p. 260). The Bible is "a true and live myth" of the incarnation.

V

The sacrament of the Word, both in the reading of Scripture and in the celebration of the Eucharist, proceeds to the response of man to the myth of the new creation.

"And here we offer and present unto thee, O Lord, our selves, our souls and bodies, to be a reasonable, holy, and living sacrifice unto thee; . . . that we, and all others who shall be partakers of this Holy Communion, may . . . be . . . made one body with him, that he may dwell in us, and we in him."

The faith and the unity of the church will always depend upon the vitality of those who partake of his presence with one another through holy communion. "If any one is in Christ, he is a new creation." (II Cor. 5:17.) Easter is not only the festival of the return of spring. It is far deeper than the festival of the exodus from Egypt and the deliverance from political tyranny. The Bible transforms the myths of space, within the cycle of the nature festivals that remain unchanged, into the myth of end-time, which affirms the power of God to make revolutions and regenerations. Easter is the celebration of the birth of the new man. It is the feast of our escape from the prison of self, with our hates and our prejudices.

We do not know what happened on the first day of the week after the death of Jesus. We do know that his friends, dismayed and in despair, who on Thursday night abandoned him and fled, now braved the same authorities who arrested and put Jesus to death, and they spread all over the Roman Empire the good news of their Master: Life is new, and love will conquer hate, and God is love.

We learn about the mechanism of guilt feeling, which makes man hate others and hate himself, but what is the scientific method by which to create these simple commodities, love and compassion? We have been taught about biochemistry, heredity, and environment, but who will show the springs of human kindness? Some ask whether they can "believe" in Easter. The question is, rather, Can we trust an omnipotent God in history? The answer depends upon whether, for us, the old loyalties to envy, resentment, vengeance, and the spirit of "getting even" have been buried on Good Friday. Some query whether the story of the resurrection is true. The answer depends, for us here and now, on whether you and I are being re-created as men and women of maturity.

The pursuit of the new is really a surrender to the Creator of the new, who affirms and confirms our true self precisely in the measure with which we discover a respect and a concern

for the self of others. The poet asks: " Sudden renewal of the
self — from where? " " If you are in Christ," answered the
tentmaker, nineteen centuries ago, " you are a new creation."
You belong to a living Reality that death itself cannot kill.

The myth of the new creation makes us look at ourselves in
a new light. We discover the happiness of giving and the thrill
of creative joy. It is in creating joy around us that we declare
our participation in the life of Christ who promised: " Lo,
I shall be with you alway, even unto the end of the world."

We cannot improvise our faith, however, at the moment of
crisis. Christian faith is not an " on-and-off " kind of perform-
ance, once a year, at Easter, for example, or just in tough moments. It is a daily attuning, in the communion of the saints —
the universal church of Christ — to the truth that mind may
not fathom but that rings true to the ear of the spirit.

Faith is the transforming of drab existence by the awareness
of a Presence in a community. We often hear that our character is marred by our destiny, but we forget that our destiny is
often the result of our character, and our character in turn reflects the company we keep at the secret level of our being.
Communion with God is so inclusive that, although we remain
perplexed and sinful beings, we are no longer in despair, and
we go ahead from existence to life. We move from fall to fall,
but also from strength to strength, waiting with the noncha-
lance of the saints for an eternity that has already begun. Immortality is not the right of mortal man, but resurrection is the
gift of creative grace. We are born mortal and reborn immortal.

VI

The sacrament of the Word in the church, with its stress
on the threefold moment of liturgical time — creation, incarnation, new creation — leads us to the Trinitarian theology.
Because we are known of God, the Father who creates, the

Son incarnate who liberates, and the Holy Spirit who re-creates, we no longer merely exist, but we live in the New Age. Nevertheless, we do not seek to escape from this earth in the pursuit of a distant heaven. We face the problems of church order, church and state, ethics at all levels of society, labor and management, nation, race, and war. Chronological time has not been swallowed up in timelessness. But, in the company of the men of faith who precede, surround, and follow us, our existence becomes a life by which we affirm creation. We regain harmony of relationships with God, self, and others. The old estrangement is bridged. The holy becomes the awe of love. In the presence of the faithful Creator, the creature accepts its own self. The Machiavellian enmity between man and woman is composed in true marriage. Sexuality becomes a delight and a responsibility. Procreation and parenthood rediscover the blessing (Gen. 1:28). Family ties, friendships, loyalties to group, nation, earth, and church, find their place in the scheme of the highest and sole allegiance. Service is a rendering of thanks. This is the meaning of the word "Eucharist."

This new life is no starry-eyed vision, for we also hear the groans and travails of creation. Sin as a lack of trust in the Creator still describes the world, the church, and me. Only the sharpness of the Bible can prevent me from turning both the Bible and the church into a new illusion of security. God, who is still tied to the wood, keeps me from returning to Egypt and to all the myths of space, including a static and safe view of the apostolic succession, sacramental validity, or Biblical revelation. Idols die hard.

As long as there remains a human agony, God strikes the hour of his terrible, compassionate, holy time.

DATE DUE

GAYLORD			PRINTED IN U.S.A.